THE HISTORY OF
CHIVALRY AND ARMOUR

THE HISTORY OF
CHIVALRY AND ARMOUR

WITH DESCRIPTIONS OF THE FEUDAL SYSTEM,
THE PRACTICES OF KNIGHTHOOD, THE TOURNAMENT,
AND TRIALS BY SINGLE COMBAT

DR. F. KOTTENKAMP
TRANSLATED BY THE REV. A. LÖWY

BRACKEN BOOKS
LONDON

THE HISTORY OF CHIVALRY AND ARMOUR
is published by Bracken Books
an imprint of Bestseller Publications Ltd.
Princess House, 50 Eastcastle Street
London W1N 7AP, England

Published by arrangement with Portland House
A Division of dilithium Press, Ltd.
distributed by Crown Publishers, Inc.
225 Park Avenue South, New York, New York 10003

First impression 1988
Copyright © 1988 by dilithium Press, Ltd.

ISBN 1 85170 236 9

Printed in Italy

FOREWORD.

The knightly virtues that comprised chivalric honour included not only the art of war, but also the generosity, gallantry, justice, and religious demeanour required by the feudal system which enforced these codes of behaviour among the European aristocracy of the Middle Ages.

The History of Chivalry and Armour tells us about the knights, their arms, ornaments, and entertainments. Reproduced from hand-coloured engravings in the original nineteenth-century edition, the lavishly detailed plates accompanying the text show us the positions and perils of the joust, the banners of the tournament, the intricate designs wrought on heavy horse-armour, the swords, daggers, and all the instruments of siege and attack. But we have as well the literature of the age of chivalry, and it is through the work of medieval poets and troubadours that the voices of the past come fully alive.

We will preface this admirable history of chivalry and armour with a note on the literature of courtly love, specifically the *Lancelot* by Chrétien de Troyes, a twelfth-century French poet considered to be the "father" of the Arthurian romance. In Chrétien's epic *Lancelot* there is an incident of judicial combat—or legal dueling—wherein we may observe the weaponry in the *History of Chivalry and Armour* as it was actually used. *Lancelot* is one version of the famous romance of Lancelot and Guinevere, King Arthur's lovely Queen, whose mutual attraction led to many difficulties for everyone, and ultimately sent Lancelot off on his quest for the Holy Grail. When blood was found on both Lancelot's and Guinevere's quite separate sheets one morning, Sir Lancelot and Sir Meleagant (on behalf of the King) fought each other for their differing accounts of the Queen's honour. This was a contest of courtly love tried through judicial combat, the legal function of chivalry. We read:

> When the oaths had been taken, their horses were brought forward, which were fair and good in every way. Each man mounts his own horse, and they ride at once at each other as fast as the steeds can carry them; and when the horses are in mid-career, the knights strike each other so fiercely that there is nothing left of the lances in their hands. Each brings the other to earth; however, they are not dismayed, but they rise at once and attack each other with their sharp drawn swords. The burning sparks fly in the air from their helmets. They assail each other so bitterly with the drawn swords in their hands that, as they thrust and draw, they encounter each other with their blows and will not pause even to catch their breath.

There are two types of romance for Chrétien: the happy and the tragic. *Lancelot* is of the latter variety. The tragic romance consists of adulterous or unequal love and comes to no good end, while the happy romance holds equivalent and licensed passions, and culminates in eventual marriage. In a tragic romance, anything may be justified by Love's commands, but one must choose whether to obey the Master. At the end of the romance, Lancelot and Guinevere, who obey their Master Love, are morally wrong in their adultery, even though Guinevere's innocence is actually proven by the outcome of the judicial combat quoted above. In both types of romance, love becomes a teacher as well as an entertainer. The codes of behaviour for all lovers—the art of courtly love—are drawn from the works of Ovid and Virgil, but adapted and embroidered to suit the strictures of a Christian society.

Chivalry and love are the two golden threads running through all of Chrétien's romances. His writings paint a brilliant portrait of the society that he lived in and served as court poet. Though he would often draw his details from real life, there is in all his work a strain of the ideal, a strain that reaches toward a society of delicate manners in search of a world impeccably (and impossibly) courteous, generous, and honourable.

It is not surprising that the art of courtly love and chivalry—the art of courtly war—both draw upon the literature and resources of classical antiquity for their foundations. In *The History of Chivalry and Armour* one finds the ancient Romans cited both as source and documentation for the articles and engines of war and the strategies necessary for their use. Alas for the age of chivalry, the invention of gunpowder and the primitive muskets that ensued soon heralded an end to an epic age of warfare. Fittingly though, this splendid book closes with text and illustrations on the tournament rather than the musket. For it was indeed a grand spectacle—the pageantry and arms of the aristocracy at play.

B. L. H. Masterson

New York City
1988

PUBLISHER'S NOTE.

The astute reader will wish to note that the text of *The History of Chivalry and Armour* was written (and translated from the German) in the middle of the nineteenth century, and that due caution must be exercised with references to such phrases as "modern times" or "the recent disturbances in the Americas." The earlier political geography and occasionally anachronistic style of spelling and hyphenation found herein should by no means distract from the splendour of this book.

TRANSLATOR'S PREFACE.

In the present work, Chivalry is described with regard to its feudal origin, its usages and ceremonies, arms, sports, and judicial combats. The pictorial illustrations are divided into two equal portions, the first of which represents ancient and mediæval weapons, with the various pieces of armour; and the other, combatants engaged in the achievements and the trials of the joust.

The Translator, without interfering with the original plan of the Author, has endeavoured to improve the practical character of the work by the addition of marginal annotations, a few foot-notes, a list of the illustrations, and an alphabetical index. He has also placed the references to the authorities at the end of the work, where they will satisfy the claims of the critical student, without inconveniencing the majority of readers, who take no interest in the enumeration of the original sources.

Such well-known authors as Du Cange, Meyrick, and others are, in most instances, mentioned without reiterating the titles of their works. The numerous references to Grimm relate to his *Deutsche Rechtsalterthümer*, or Antiquities of Germanic Law. They will prove valuable additions to the history of a bygone state of society, and help to present chivalry in a variety of interesting aspects.

A. LÖWY.

CONTENTS.

LIST OF PLATES.

SKETCH OF THE FEUDAL SYSTEM.

Chivalry and Feudalism. CHIVALRY and its military duties originated in the institution of aristocracy, and exhibited during the middle ages, those social and political relations of the nobility, which, in a greater or smaller extent, distinguished the privileged classes of all Germanic nations.

German Nobility. It is undoubted that these privileged classes existed among the Germans before the invasion of the Roman empire. They are mentioned by Tacitus in various places, under the designation of "nobiles," or "principes," in contradistinction to the plebeian orders. Later records, legal and historical, of German tribes settled in the provinces of the western empire, treat likewise of aristocracy as a class distinct from that of mere freemen. In the ancient laws, the *weregild*, or fine paid by the murderer to the relations of the slain, was rated higher, if the victim was of noble origin. In historical works, there are also allusions to noble families **Aristocratic Families.** that belonged to various German tribes. Among the Goths are noticed the Amali and the Balti; among the Franks, the Merovingians; among the Lombards, the Gungici; among the Bavarians, the Agilolfingi, &c. In the Edda, (the mythological traditions of the Scandinavians) a line of demarcation is drawn between the noble and the ignoble.* We thus obtain from various independent testimonies, the convincing proof, that the institution of nobility was inherent in the national economy of the early Germans.

Prerogatives. Nobility in all instances, is invested with characteristic prerogative. What was the nature of those prerogatives among the Germans cannot be clearly determined; but we learn from a statement of Tacitus, that the chieftains of their tribes were elected from the higher ranks. Thus, the Cherusci petitioned the emperor Claudius to restore to them, as their leader, the last survivor of their nobles. This application suggests, that the high-born were considered as the kindred and peers of royalty, and exercised greater authority than the mere freemen.

Sacerdotal Functions of the Nobility. The nobles combined with their duties, the functions of priests, to which, in some instances, judicial power was also attached, as we are led to infer from Scandinavian testimonies of the tenth century. In Iceland, the heathen sacerdotal dignitaries, termed Godar,* held both religious and judicial offices, and transmitted their dignity to their male heirs. The Godar presided at the judicial court and at ritual ceremonies, appointed their coadjutors in the administration of justice, officiated at communal solemnities, (such as the manumission of slaves), and watched over the preservation of public security and peace. This combination of duties is nearly analogous to the several functions which Tacitus ascribes to the German priests.

Their Political Influence. The nobles were also charged with important political affairs, as is attested by Roman writers who lived during the decline of the empire. On embracing Christianity, the priestly immunities of the nobility were, of course, either lost, or appropriated by the Roman clergy; but the nobles still retained the direction of the judicial administration, as is to be observed in the first establishment of the large German domains, among the Franks, Saxons, Alemanni, &c. Judges were, in the days of Tacitus, elected by the assembly of the people; after the great migration, however, when the Germans began to form their extensive realms, the appointment of judges seems to have devolved upon the kings. In this way, the latter nominated their *Grafen*, (reeves, **Graf, or Count.** counts). The Romans translated the word Graf by *Comes*, which, at the final period of their empire, corresponded in meaning with *præses provinciæ*, (the governor of a province). The word *comes*, which was modified in the several Romanesque languages,

---

* In the Rigsmál, (or song of Rig) the servile class, the freemen, and the nobles, are derived from three different ancestors. The ill-favored THRÆL, (*i.e.*, the enthralled) is the son of Aï and Edda. KARL, (*i. e.*, Man) the lively son of Afi and Amma, is the ancestor of the free landholders. It is remarkable that the fall of free men into servitude, is indicated by the change of the word Karl into the opprobrious English terms *carle* and *churl*. JARL, (*i. e.*, Noble, with which the title of *Earl* is connected), is the son of Father and Mother. He is the ancestor of the aristocracy. The Rigsmál says of him :—

> "Light are his locks,   His piercing eyes
> And bright his cheeks,   Are aiming serpents."—TR.

---

* Godar is the plural of Godi, a divine.—TR.

(*comte, conte, conde*=count), signified, at a later time, a certain grade of feudal nobility.

The dignity of count appears to have been conferred exclusively Duties of the Counts. on nobles, and was not merely connected with the chief direction of the courts of law, but likewise with the civil administration. The Gothic counts superintended the revenue derived from the Romans, the convocation of the people to the annual muster, the maintenance of public tranquillity, &c.

It is not a settled question, whether the nobles, at the division Allotment of Lands. of lands wrested from the Romans, received larger allotments than the freemen; but it is consonant with the nature of regal authority, that a preference should be shown in favour of the former. The king surrounded himself with a number of officials, (*ministeriales*) whose services in the camp and at the court, were rewarded by the grant of so-called fiscal, or crown-lands. Noble courtiers, according to Tacitus, did not disdain to perform such menial services for royalty, as would, among the Romans, have been assigned to slaves. At the court of the Frankish kings, the nobles bore the title of Antrustiones*; and they, like their Antrustiones. sovereigns, gathered around them followers, who were composed of freemen and dependants. Neither were these courtly offices intrusted to nobles only. The Salic law speaks of freemen and even Romans, promoted to such high places. After the middle of the sixth century, these followers attained a preponderating influence at the courts of their princes, and subsequently effected a complete revolution in the allegiance of the nobles to the crown, and in the position of the alodialists, or freeholders. Like the Franks, the Goths had their suite of nobles. The Visigothic King Ricimer appeared on solemn occasions, with noble courtiers (*reguli*), who then already displayed in their equipment and arms that pageant, which remained the fashion throughout the middle ages.

Pride of ancestry is a natural concomitant of aristocracy, and is Pedigree. observable in the very dawn of German history. The advantages of high birth were impressed upon youths in the days of Tacitus, no less than in a later age, when German kingdoms

* Antrustiones is the Latinized plural of the Frankish title of Antrustio, *i.e.*, the trusty officer, or he who is in the confidence of the King. The Salic law describes him as "eum qui *in truste dominica est*."—Tr.

sprang up from the ruins of the Roman empire. The Goths, in particular, were remarkably proud of their pedigrees, and bequeathed their high notions of birth to the Spaniards, as a prominent feature of their national character. Much stress was laid by Theodoric upon the fact of his being a descendant of the Amali. Nor was it considered a matter of little moment, that Cassiodorus was enabled to enrich his pedigree by the addition of a few ancestral names.

We have no information respecting the early signs of distinction between nobles and freemen. To judge by the illustrations Badges of Distinction. of the Sachsenspiegel,* chaplets on the heads of kings and nobles seem to have served as indications of superior rank. In the advanced period of the middle ages, coronets marked the several grades of feudal aristocracy, and possibly, were intended as improvements upon the simple decorations of antiquity. According to Jornandes, the noble Goths were recognizable by their hats. They also wore golden rings on their fingers; and it was by this ornament, that the noblemen fallen at the battle of Xeres de la Frontera† were distinguishable from the rest of the killed. Other signs of high rank belong to a later period.

The mass of the German nation consisted of freemen, who had the same rights as the nobles, if we except the above-mentioned Freemen. privileges. They were unrestricted in the tenure of their lands, in the power of alienating the same, and in the choice of their settlements within the limits of the empire. Their property entitled them to assist in the proceedings of justice, and to have their share of legislative authority in the annual meetings of the people. They were also at liberty to carry arms and to make use of them in avenging injuries done to their person, honor, or property, if they preferred vengeance to the acceptance of the pecuniary fine, fixed by the law. This right of feud, or retaliation, was afterwards Feud. claimed by the aristocracy, as their exclusive privilege. Among the Scandinavian freeholders, it remained in force till late in the middle

* The Sachsenspiegel is a compilation of laws and customs, which, during the middle ages were in force in Germany, and more particularly in Saxony. The collection was made by a Saxon nobleman about the year 1215, and consists of two parts: the code of civil law, (Landrecht) and of feudal law, (Lehenrecht).—Tr.

† The victory there gained by the Arabs in 711 put an end to the dominion of the Goths in Spain.—Tr.

ages, when the free classes of the other European states had already been reduced to a more or less oppressive state of servitude. The rights of the free landowners involved the duty of joining the Heribannum.* While employed in this military service, the freeman had his indisputable share in the plunder. He was also exempt from the burdens of taxation and from the compulsory labour of tributary subjects. He had to pay no permanent ground-rent, with which only the subjected Romans were charged. The dues demanded of the freeman were merely of a temporary nature, and consisted of presents and supplies to the king and his court. In times of war, he had also to provide horses and waggons. The freemen, among each other, constituted communal associations for the mutual protection of their rights. As an outward sign of their independence, they wore their hair long, like the nobles.

Heribannum.

The circumstances which conspired to deprive the free landholders of their independent condition can be traced in historical events, in the state of society, and in the effect of legal enactments. The franchises, once possessed by the free multitude of the people, were gradually usurped by the comparatively few families of the feudal aristocracy, while the majority of the once free classes were subjected to a state of villenage or servitude. The condition of dependence, like the circumstances by which it had been adduced, materially varied in degree, and cannot be minutely described here, the subject being too remote from our purpose. The following few words will suffice to show the contrast between hereditary villenage and the hereditary rank of nobility.

Decline of Freedom.

No villein possessed an unlimited right of acquiring property; he was not allowed to remove from the locality assigned to him by his lord; he was excluded from taking an active part in the administration of the law, and from voting at the national assemblies; he was not permitted to carry arms, and only followed the armed bands of warriors for the purpose of escorting the wounded and burying the dead; at the same time the law refused him the use of the sword, the lance, and the shield. He had to perform compulsory labour in the house and the field of his lord, and to pay a variety of taxes. Moreover, it was his duty to supply provisions for the army and food for the horses; to keep the weapons of the warriors in good

Liti, or Villeins.

condition, forge horses' shoes, &c. The free proprietors kept so completely aloof from the Liti (*i. e.*, villeins)* that even in the ancient northern mythology, a special region is assigned, in after life, to the dependent labourers. As a striking mark of inferiority, the servile classes were obliged to wear their hair short-cropped, so as to avoid all equality with the dominant party.

The feudal nobles, as we have noticed, succeeded the free landholders in the possession of former privileges. The origin of this class of aristocracy has been ascribed to the courtly followers of royalty, the Antrustiones of the Franks. These dignitaries received royal lands in lieu of pay; perhaps, at first, only for life-time, but afterwards as hereditary property. The weakness of the Merovingian dynasty certainly leads to the supposition, that reversionary grants of land could not easily be recovered by the crown, and remained at last in possession of the beneficed tenants by the force of prescription. In 887, Charles the Bald rendered the dignity of the counts inheritable by royal edict; yet the wording of the law sufficiently shows that it merely sanctioned an old-established usage. The perpetuation of territorial grants, while materially diminishing the influence of the crown upon the holder of the property, changed altogether the character of the original donation. Such landed property, first held by high officers of the crown, and afterwards, as the heirloom of certain families, was originally termed a "benefice" (*beneficium*), and subsequently, a fee or feud (*feudum*). Even in the days of Charlemagne, such tenures were already very numerous, and distinguished from lands · held by freemen. The Capitularies† of that monarch abound in passages relative to feudal tenures; the one cited in the note is of especial interest, for the early mention it makes of cavaliers‖ (*caballarii*), who

Feudalism.

Feudal Tenure.

---

* The *Liti* or *Lidi* (also *Læti* and *Leti*, and in the Lombardian laws, *Aldiones*), constituted the lowest order of rural labourers. Grimm connects this word with the old German *Laz*, (*i, e.*, lazy), as a degrading appellation of the servile classes Is it not likely that this mediæval word was borrowed from the Slavonians, whose name and unpopularity supplied the European nations with the designation of *Slave?* The term for "people" is in Russian, *Luedi*, in Bohemian, *Lidé.*—Tr.

† Capitularies, or decrees of Frankish rulers, commence with the reign of Charles Martel, and end with that of Louis the Pious. The collection was commenced in the 9th Century, and owes its name to its division into small chapters *(Capitularia)*.—Tr.

‖ *Comites* et *vasalli* nostri, qui *beneficia* habere noscuntur et *Caballarii* omnes ad placitum nostrum veniant bene præparati.—Baluzii, Capitularia, A.D. 807, Tom. I., p. 460.

---

* Heribannum means the order or summons (bannum) to join the army.—Tr.

will come under our notice under the more expressive title of knights.

An erroneous opinion was formerly prevalent, that feudal nobility Romans and Barbarians. had been bestowed solely upon German functionaries, established in the provinces taken from the Romans. The latter were not disqualified from holding fiefs. It can easily be conceived, that there were many official employments to which the victorious barbarians were not suited, and to which, in consequence, Romans were appointed. Thus Cassiodorus occupied an eminent post during the Ostrogothic dominion in Italy. Also among the Visigoths, in the south of Gaul and in Spain, Romans held places under Government, as we learn from Sidonius Apollinaris. The Frankish laws speak very distinctly of the Romans attached to the court, designating them *convivæ regis* (men admitted to the royal table). Their *weregild* was fixed at the rate of one third beyond that of an alodialist. Nor were the Romans excluded from military service. In the victory of Clovis over the Visigoths, the son of the Roman author Sidonius Apollinaris fell by the side of the nobles of Auvergne, while fighting at the head of the Gothic army. The Salic law likewise alludes to Romans serving in the army. Through military service they had a chance of rising from their low degree of tributary dependence to the position of their free fellow-combatants. In addition to these circumstances, so favorable to the subjected Romans, their clergy must have exercised a considerable sway over Roman Clergy. the Franks, the Goths, and the Lombards ; and on the conversion of the latter two tribes to the Catholic faith, the religious teachers of Rome, undoubtedly, had good opportunities of raising their own kindred from the degraded position of a vanquished people.

The Antrustiones, as has been noticed, had their followers, who Retainers. were composed of freemen and villeins. Indeed, it appears to have been part of their duties, to attach to themselves such men, so that they might be able to supply the numbers required for the levies of the army. The holders of large fiefs or benefices, extended their power by letting portions of their estate to other noblemen or freemen. By such a transfer of tenure, their tenants were bound to a performance of duties and services, and were placed in a state of dependency analogous to the allegiance they themselves owed to the crown. This process of making grants out of estates held under the crown was called *sub-infeudation*, and is Sub-infeudation. referred to in the capitularies of Pepin and Charlemagne.

In the tenth century, this mode of transferring landed property had become so general, that nearly all fees were held in sub-infeudation. The same homage and oath of fidelity were offered by the tenant,— now termed vassal,—to the chief holder of lands (the lord who held *in chief*), as this one had offered to the sovereign. Owing to the complicated relations arising from such grants, new burdens and personal duties were imposed, which made great inroads on the rights of alodial proprietors.

The alodialists were deprived of their liberty, partly by events subversive to their social position, and partly by the force Causes of Declining Freedom. of legal enactments. A brief outline of the causes which brought about such a revolution will explain this subject. The dissolution of the Frankish empire, under the successors of Charlemagne, which effected vital changes in the condition in France, Germany, and Italy, had been already provoked during the reign of that monarch. Laws enacted during his lifetime, strove to remedy the blunders and the negligence of the provincial governors (the counts), who felt no scruple in oppressing the petty landholders, and in making constant encroachments on the fiscal lands, situated within their jurisdiction. The undue power of high officials endangered both the authority of the crown and the independence of the freemen. During the whole reign of Charlemagne, the latter were compelled to neglect their lands, and to attend to the harassing duties of the camp, without receiving a fair compensation for their services. At the same time, the freeman had to provide himself with arms and food, and to furnish supplies towards the common necessities. The chances of plunder might have afforded some compensation to the ruined soldier for his loss of time and labor, but they were too few and insignificant in the wars with the Saxons and Lombards, since both nations were to be left in the unmolested enjoyment of their possessions and privileges. To escape the oppressiveness of military duty, many freemen entered the clerical profession. The emperor, anxious to mitigate the growing evil, had to concede to his military servants the necessary relief, by the extension of benefices.

During the incessant conflicts of civil war after the death of Charlemagne, the condition of the alodialists, or free holders of property, became much worse. They were now abandoned to the misrule of the governing counts, who, unchecked by any superior authority, committed all sorts of arbitrary excesses, took unlawful possession of crown lands, disregarded the time-honoured forms of judicial proceedings and of national assemblies. At that period of domestic and national warfare, when unabated hostilities raged in every district of France, and when the rights of the sovereign and the people were alternately trodden under foot, the alodial proprietors were neither able to perform their military obligations, nor to interpose resistance to the unfair practices of the parties in power.

Arbitrary Conduct of the Counts.

To rescue some pittance from universal ruin, they were constrained to sacrifice their freedom and seek the protection of opulent and powerful proprietors, whose aid could only be purchased at the price of more or less galling servitude. The labouring classes, consisting principally of agriculturists, dragged the entire mass of the defenceless people into their own state of dependence.

Submission of the Freemen.

With the loss of personal rights the extinction of political privileges kept even pace. We have observed, that the freemen were entitled to take an active part in the public assemblies, and that without their consent, no decision, involving national interests, could pass into law. During the reign of Charlemagne and his early successors, the approving vote of the people was duly obtained. Even fifty years after Charlemagne, Charles the Bald acknowledged this ancient principle:—" The law is made by the people's consent to the resolution of the king."* Soon afterwards, this legislative co-operation of the people was dispensed with.

Extinction of ancient privileges.

In 882, the last laws were issued by Carloman, in which those national rights are avowed. The disenfranchisement of the French freemen may therefore be dated from this period, and then must have commenced the division of the realm into groups or fiefs, which became much more conspicuous in the tenth and eleventh centuries. Freeholds were now so generally supplanted by feudal grants, as to give rise to the legal maxim, which remained

Decline of Freedom in France.

in force till the outbreak of the revolution :—" Nulle terre sans seigneur," (No land without a *Lord*).

In Germany, this great change was not effected at such an early date, or by any sweeping process. In different parts of the land, the communities of free peasants retained their independence, as for instance, in Friesland, Westphalia, Swabia, &c. The feudal nobles, selfishly encroaching on the rights of the crown, as well as on the social and political claims of the people, were for a time kept in check by the superior power of the emperors, until the nobility and the clergy triumphed over the defeated exertions of the rulers. The lawlessness and confusion which extended to the reign of Henry I.* favored the usurpations of the feudal nobles. Their sway, and the whole system of their pretensions, were so firmly established during the intestine wars in the reign of Henry IV.,† that only a small fraction of the former freemen could retain the ancient privileges. In addition to the disastrous state of the empire, other causes of an anti-social character helped to undermine the security, and at last to put an end to the existence of free landowners.

Decline of Freedom in Germany.

The most prominent evil was the right of feud or blood-revenge, in which monarchs and free subjects were apt to indulge, and which, ultimately, became a distinct and exclusive right of the aristocracy. All freemen laid claim to the right of avenging injuries done to life, limb, honor, or estate. This right might be exercised in person or by proxy, if the offended party refused to accept, or if the offender failed to offer the prescribed pecuniary fine. This barbarous revenge produced a perpetual insecurity of life and property. The consequence was, that men had to seek the protection of some mighty feudal lord, in order to escape harassing and vexatious tyranny.

The right of Feud.

In England, the right of blood-revenge seems to have been as fierce and productive of turbulence as in France and Germany. After the Conquest, the landed property was held by comparatively few nobles, while the mass of freemen fell into a state of dependence, though their condition, on the whole, was not as

England.

---

* " Lex consensu populi fit constitutione regis."—Recueil des Historiens, (Bouquet) VII., 656.

* Henry I. (commonly called the Fowler), was the first German King of the Saxon House. His reign lasted from 919 to 936. He built many fortified cities, and compelled every ninth freeholder, who was liable to serve in the army, to settle in one of the towns. —Tr.

† Henry IV. was German Emperor from 1056 to 1106.—Tr.

degraded as that of the enthralled classes on the Continent; still they did not escape exactions, menial labour, and deprivations of personal rights.

Besides the practice of self-revenge, there existed other customs German Customs. founded on German laws, which had the tendency of subjecting the people to the debasement of serfdom. The following were the most conspicuous:—

I.—A freeman, marrying a woman of inferior birth, fell into Marriage. servitude. This custom, though not universal, was in force among the Franks, and gave rise to the axiom laid down in subsequent French jurisprudence:—"En formariage, le pire emporte le bon," (in case of an unequal match, the low person debases the high-born); this rule was observed by the Alemanni and the Danes. Among the majority of the Germans, and among the Anglo-Saxons, the issue of unequal marriages was doomed to servitude. It was only in the reign of the Emperor Frederic I.,* that a law was enacted which secured freedom to the children born of a plebeian mother. The Swedes alone pursued, in this respect, a more considerate system.

II.—An alien, after having taken up his abode in a locality for a Immigrants. year and a day, lost his freedom. He was subjected to a similar loss of liberty if he worked together with serfs, or resided with them under the same roof. This legal custom, which was upheld during the complications of general war, tended to injure the rights of those, who had spent a year in a different dukedom or county, or even in a different parish. Fugitives lost their freedom, if, within that short space of time, they did not return to their former homes. The feudal nobility, by such a state of laws, acquired increased influence and gained new subjects, whilst their strongholds became places of refuge for those who were in search of safe protection.

III.—Freemen who did not attend to the summons of serving in Absence from the Heribannum. the army, lost their privileges. Pecuniary fines, were, in some instances, accepted in lieu of military service. Among the Anglo-Saxons, alodial lands (bocland) were, in cases of desertion, confiscated by the kings, and then mostly appropriated by the counts.

* Frederic I. (Barbarossa) occupied the throne of German Emperors from 1152 to 1190. —Tr.

IV.—A freeman unable to pay the due weregild, (composition for manslaughter) was, according to some legal customs, bound Inability to pay the Weregild. to suffer his wife and children to go into slavery, and had to forfeit his own freedom.

V.—Prisoners of war became slaves and base menials. In this manner, non-Germans were enslaved; as for example, the Prisoners of War. Sclavonians, whose national name has supplied the English, the German, and the Romanesque languages, with the term *Slave*, (Sklave, Esclave, Schiavo, &c.), as expressive of the lowest degree of servitude. Subjection of the same description awaited the Germans themselves, if, in war, they became the prisoners of other Germans. Thus Jornandes relates of the Goths, that they made slaves of their prisoners, the Quadi. This method of treating the vanquished was only abandoned, when the aristocratic classes renounced their coarse habits, and allowed themselves to be guided by an improved sense of justice and generosity. It was chivalry that put an end to such inhuman and irreligious proceedings. A knight, who was made prisoner, paid a ransom, or offered some satisfactory security, and was then dismissed, or only carried off as an hostage, without losing his personal freedom.

VI.—Men, actuated by peculiar and diverse motives, used, on their own accord, to surrender their independence to others. Voluntary Subjection. Even Tacitus mentions instances in which Germans, when under the influence of the maddening passion of gambling, staked and lost their freedom. During the utter confusion which succeeded the reign of Charlemagne, many freemen readily resigned their independent position, as will hereafter be more fully stated.

Causes like those we have enumerated, had deprived about half of the rural population of France of their liberty, before the abolition of freedom became universal. With regard to the earlier condition of Germany, Grimm, in his Rechtsalterthümer, p. 331, assumes that the loss of liberty took place in a similar ratio.

We must also advert to another important cause of the substitution of feudalism for the freehold system. The mode of armament and the nature of tactics had, even before Charlemagne, undergone reforms which were more fully developed in the tenth century. Horsemen in armour, replacing the infantry forces of freemen, began to decide the issue of battles, and wrought complete changes in military enterprise.

The Germans were not the originators of heavy cavalry, but formed it in imitation of the Roman troops. Towards the decline of the empire, when the legions, which once constituted the overwhelming force of the army, had become completely demoralised, the emperors learnt of the eastern barbarians, the use of heavy cavalry, in which both horses and men were covered by iron sheathings. The riders were protected in such a manner, as to retain the free exercise of their limbs. Under Constantine the Great, such cavalry formed already an essential part of the army. Thus, for example, it formed the main part of the troops, which fought under Maxentius, in the Battle of Turin. Whenever they had an opportunity to execute an attack in close column, they were irresistible. Subsequently, however, when discipline became gradually relaxed, they refused to wear heavy armour, just as the legionary foot soldiers, ever since the time of the Emperor Gratian, had refused the heavy arms of defence, in consequence of their being too cumbersome. The horsemen of the Goths, the Alani, and the Huns, on the other hand, copied from the Romans the use of heavy armour, and they thereby gained considerable advantage over their opponents; so much so, that a Roman author, who lived at the termination of the empire, attributes to that particular circumstance, the cause of the constant successes of the barbarians.

Heavy-armed German Cavalry.

The Franks, too, at the very commencement, appear to have adopted this species of defensive armour, so that in the battle against the Visigoths, Clovis escaped death through the protection of such solid coverings. In the days of Charlemagne, heavy cavalry, it is believed, formed a considerable portion of the army. This service in heavy armour was then already connected with the possession of certain benefices or fiefs, and horsemen were separately mentioned in the summons to enlist in the army. This is to be inferred from an allusion to *caballarii* in the capitularies of the year 807.* The expense of purchasing a horse, and equipping it, as also the charge of keeping the necessary number of attendants, were beyond the means of common freemen, who, in consequence, could not join the cavalry forces, particularly as no regular pay was given to the soldier.

Franks in Heavy Armour.

* See Note, p. 6.

In order to meet the expenses of war, crown lands were granted as benefices, under the condition that special suit and service should be rendered to the Lord paramount; just as the tenure of freehold land had, at a former period, involved the obligation of joining the military levies. The nobles, having mainly to support the burden of warfare, now claimed the right of wearing arms, as an exclusive privilege. In the same manner, had the freemen, in contradistinction to the dependent classes, once enjoyed the special privilege of carrying shields, swords, and lances, and of serving in military expeditions.

Feudal Grants.

In Germany, the mounted service of the nobles became general during the reign of Henry the Fowler, and it was the heavy-armed cavalry that gave to the Germans the preponderance over the Hungarians. Military troops of this description, may have existed before that time, but, at all events, they formed the chief power of the nation during the 11th century, when the levy of freemen had been abolished. According to Du Cange, (voce *Miles*), only the noble horseman or knight, was designated by the term Soldier, which was no longer applied to the inferior grades of combatants. The word *caballarius,* as contained in the capitularies, designates in all the Romanesque languages, the rank or dignity solely attainable by men of noble origin, or by those who had been promoted to the station of nobility (hence the origin of the terms *chevalier, caballero, &c*).

Heavy-armed Cavalry.

It cannot be determined, whether the feudal aristocracy, which was established by the concurrence of those circumstances, derived its origin from the nobles of the ancient Germans; for, with regard to the high families of the middle ages, as well as to those of the present day, their ancestors with but very few exceptions, cannot be traced to a remote period of antiquity. In France, there was only one family, the Périgords, that could trace its ancestry so far back as the day of Charles the Bald. In Spain, the families of Guzman and Ponce de Leon were the only ones who could exhibit a pedigree which dated back to the times of the Visigothic Kings. The statements concerning the origin of other families,—for instance, that of the Montmorencies,—rest on fables which, in point of credibility, are comparable with the romances of chivalry. In Germany, even the ruling dynasties do not reach with any positive certainty, below

Pedigrees.

the 10th century. So in England, no vestige of the ancient Saxon nobility of the Thanes is discoverable in the present aristocracy, nor can the Lombard families of Italy claim a more remote antiquity.

Although no evidence exists in regard to the connection of the The Ancient and the Feudal Nobility. feudal nobility with the nobles of the Germanic tribes, yet such a connection may, with a high degree of plausibility, be inferred from the nature of the above-mentioned laws. There is also room for the supposition, that at the abolition of freedom, some freemen, the wealthiest and most powerful, at least, maintained the superiority of their influence, and became feudal lords by taking men of inferior position under their protection.

While men of lower birth were rising in rank, families whose Rise and Fall of Nobles. nobility was more ancient than the feudal system, grew poor, and consequently, were lost in the multitude of the commonalty. Among the Franks, aristocratic prerogatives, in all probability, ceased with the loss of territorial possessions. The same was certainly the case with the ancient Saxon nobility of England.

The existence of an aristocracy without a surname cannot be well Surnames. conceived; a general adoption of such names must have taken place after the occurrence of that change by which the nobles isolated themselves from the common people; but it cannot be determined at what particular time the aristocracy resorted to the adoption of a distinctive appellation. Evidences of this adoption of surnames can only be traced to the 12th century, and this accounts for the fact, that but a few families can boast of a more remote antiquity.

At first, a single name sufficed to identify an individual, whether freeborn or noble; confusion having been obviated by the great number of German proper names. The names assumed at a later period were chiefly derived from the designations of family estates, a custom which was coeval with the institution of feudal nobility, but which only became general in the 13th century.

Another distinctive sign of noble families, the so-called coat-of-arms, Coat of Arms. was also introduced in a gradual manner. There is no doubt that banners and shields had, in distant ages, been marked with emblematic representations. The Saxons, for instance, in the time of Charlemagne, adopted the horse as their emblem. Still, there seems to be no reliable evidence that hereditary coats-of-arms were in use during the 12th century, except in some of the royal houses or among those nobles whose authority was on an equality with royalty. The introduction of such pictorial representation has been ascribed, partly, to the usages at tournaments, in which combatants made themselves conspicuous by significant emblems; even to the time of the Crusades, when many distinguishing insignia on the banners and arms became necessary among warriors, who represented different nations and languages, and who, moreover, were but loosely kept together under their several leaders.

Feudal nobility, constituted by the tenure of property, and by the protection afforded to inferiors, had been established by a Nobility by Charter. conjuncture of events and by self-nomination. When the nobility had separated itself from the ranks of the people, and had assumed the exclusiveness of a privileged class of men, the princes began to exercise, as a particular sign of their authority, the right of granting nobility to men who owned no territorial possessions. In France, this royal prerogative of conferring the rank of nobility seems to have been used after the fall of the Carlovingian dynasty. It could only be exercised when the supreme power regained new force under the successors of Hugh Capet. The first charters of nobility were granted by Philip the Bold about the year 1272. In the reigns of Philip the Fair and his sons, these demonstrations of royal favour happened more frequently.

The institution of knighthood, also, was the cause of a large accession to the numbers of the existing aristocracy. In some countries, men, knighted according to the prescribed rules, possessed full claims to the privileges of the noble.

The so-called German Briefadel, (nobility *by writ*) appears to have been chiefly established by the minor princes, who were Nobles without Lands. anxious to arrest the decline of their authority. Traces of promotion to nobility without property, it must be observed, occur in the reign of the German Emperors, even in the 12th and 13th centuries. It has been noticed that the feudal nobility succeeded the freemen in their immunities, as well as in their legal obligations; hence, the nobles laboured under the same restrictions as the freemen in regard to their marriages. Just as the intermarriage of the free-born with a serf, resulted in the loss of certain rights, so the misalliances of the nobles proved detrimental to their peculiar privileges.

In Germany, the issue of a debasing marriage could hold no land immediately under the sovereign. In France, although admitted to their inheritance and to knighthood, they were, in other respects, considered as Bastards, until a charter of nobility reinstated them in their paternal rank. The same unrestricted right which the freeman had enjoyed in his property, was probably enjoyed also by the first feudal lord; it was only at a later period, that those reservations and exactions were introduced, which were demanded under the titles of reliefs, fines, &c. Compared with other landholders, the feudal nobles, at all events, possessed the most extensive liberties. The French nobility, for example, was, previously to the outbreak of the first Revolution, exempted from the regular ground-rent.

Debasing Marriages.

The free-born men, to the exclusion of the serfs, had been entitled to a share in civil and judicial administration, but now they were altogether supplanted by the feudal nobles, who represented the nation in the assembly of the estates, and took into their hands the power of enforcing justice. This was the case in France during the reign of the first kings of the Capet dynasty.

Civil Rights of the Feudal Nobles.

An account of the subsequent condition of the citizens, both in France and in Germany, is beyond the sphere of this essay, which is merely intended to point out the connection that existed between the feudal nobility and the classes originally free. The political rights of the latter have only remained intact in Sweden and in Norway, where the estate of the peasantry is represented in the national assemblies. The freemen, in contradistinction to those in bondage, had, before the feudal period, been entitled to carry arms and to appear with the shield, the sword, and the spear. In the same manner, the feudal nobility claimed, as their exclusive right, the performance of equestrian martial service.

Even in the latest period of the middle ages, the freemen and also the patricians of French and German cities were excluded from performing knightly services, and from taking an active part in the tournaments, &c. Among the exclusive privileges of the nobility we mention, lastly, the right of feud which, in Germany and in France, prevailed to a great extent. In England, after the Norman Conquest, the legislature ignored this right, but in France it was legally noticed and placed within narrower limits in the code of the Ninth Louis. In the reign of Louis XI., whose authority rested on a more solid basis, this feudal right altogether ceased. In Germany, it was abolished under the Emperor Maximilian.

Feudalism, in regard to its origin and its forms, was devised to enhance the regal power, the vassal being bound to the sovereign, of whom he held estates, by the vows of submission and fealty, which compelled him to perform certain services. But it is an acknowledged fact, that everywhere except in England, this system baffled the expectations of the monarchs. In France, after the administration of Charlemagne, the last Carlovingian rulers had less power, and were more indigent, than the least of their vassals. A thorough centralisation of the monarchy could only be effected after the lapse of many centuries. In Germany, also, the authority of the emperors endured so many shocks from the feudal party, that ultimately, the highest title of the empire was reduced to a mere cypher, and the empire itself, while broken up into countless petty sovereignties, was unable to check internal differences, or to resist foreign aggression.

Feudalism dangerous to Monarchy.

In the foregoing outline, we have sketched the origin of nobility both in France and in Germany. Other contingencies regulated the establishment and the peculiar position of the nobility in England, in Spain, and in Italy.

In England, owing to the Conquest, most of the ancient Saxon nobles had either perished or been lost in the mass of the people. They were replaced by the Normans of the victorious Duke, and by the numerous adventurers who had been drafted from France, Germany, Flanders, and Spain, to serve under the banner of the invader. Nearly all lands were transferred to new proprietors, chiefly followers of the conqueror. These were invested with fiefs on the principle of the Norman feudal law, with these differences, however, that the ancestral position of the vassal was not taken into consideration, and that the oath of allegiance was required, both of those who held *in chief*, and of their tenants. Thus the principle on which the English nobility was founded, underwent a thorough change, which was not ascribable to any turbulence of the free, or to the necessity of protecting the defenceless subjects; but mainly to the scheme of maintaining a cruel conquest by the help of its

England.

willing instruments. The king had at his disposal the numerous horsemen of his feudal barons, who were kept in awe by cunningly devised restrictions. He chiefly relied on his standing army of mercenaries, who had been collected in all parts of Christian Europe, and were supported by the aid of incessant exactions. His arbitrary measures, rigidly enforced, proved of service even to his unenergetic successors. It was fortunate that the pressure of his unrelenting despotism soon became equally irksome to the victorious Normans and the subjected Saxons; so that both parties were anxious to unite in self-defence. It is not our object to give an account of the historical occurrences of that period; we have merely to observe, that an approach of the era of *Magna Charta* may be discerned in the dismissal of the chancellor of Richard Cœur de Lion. The civil wars in the reign of Henry III. helped to consolidate the provisions of *Magna Charta*, and ended with the constitution of a house of parliament. Mutual concessions, a gradual blending, and at last, a complete amalgamation of Saxon and Norman interests prevented that isolation of the aristocracy from the people, which took place on the Continent. This led to the prominent characteristic of England's social condition—the members of privileged classes were incorporated in the order of the so-called gentry.

In France and Germany, birth, landed property, administrative functions, and votes in the election of the sovereign, had the effect of establishing an exclusive aristocracy, but no such effect made itself felt in England. In France, the terms *noble* and *gentilhomme* were identical, but in England, the law took no cognizance of the " gentleman." If we omit some of the prerogatives of high feudal nobles (who, in parliament and in courts of justice, claimed, under the name of peers, certain political and judicial rights), the legal liberties of the people were as complete in the age of Henry III. as they are at the present time. Since the days of that monarch, continental serfdom and villenage have disappeared in England, and every successive generation has helped to obliterate the traces of dependence. Intermarriages between the noble and the ignoble classes were, most likely, never opposed by custom; and no loss of aristocratic prerogatives accrued to the children sprung from unequally matched parents. The acquisition of estates was open to all grades of the people, though the alienation and the devolution of property were limited by various provisions of feudal origin. High feudatories were bound to pay the taxes imposed upon the community at large. Most remarkable was the provision which determined that the peerage devolved on that individual who succeeded to the actual possession of the fee. In every other country, all descendants of a nobleman must needs be noble; in England, however, the principle that a peer ennobles his family was of heraldic but not of legal validity. To conditions of this kind, England owed its progressive improvement during the middle ages, no less than at the present time; and its very trials, though pernicious for the moment, never produced deep-rooted and enduring evils. The actual power and wealth of England are, in fact, the results of its constitution.

We now proceed to examine the condition of the nobles in Spain. In the Visigothic empire, the freeholders, in spite of mutual collisions and conflicts, remained independent until the invasion of Spain by the Arabs; and they do not seem to have, at any time, fallen into a state of complete abasement. When the battle in 711 decided the fate of the Gothic monarchy, the former distinctions of rank disappeared. The Christians in the Moorish dominion were placed in the condition of tributary rayahs, who, on payment of certain taxes, were allowed to remain in the land, and were treated by their rulers as an inferior class of people. In the northern provinces, also, where Christians asserted their footing by the force of arms, general misery and common calamities apparently levelled the differences of rank. Every man capable of bearing arms was incessantly employed in a military capacity, and thereby escaped servitude. Only those who were of pure Christian origin, whether of Gothic or Roman blood, seem to have been admitted to the order of nobility, though in the popular opinion of a later age, Gothic ancestors afforded a superior lustre. It is possible that the northern mountains sheltered within their range the unsubjected remnants of the warlike nobles and freemen of the Goths; so that the inhabitants of the Asturias, Gallicia, the north part of Old Castile, and Leon, are entitled to claim the honour of an unblemished origin; but this does not hold good with regard to the majority of the Spanish nobility, since many of its members, at a later period, traced their descent from Roman provincials. In any case, the inhabitants of the Asturias,

Spain.

of the greater part of Gallicia, of Leon, and Old Castile, were considered noble, without regard to freehold or feudal tenure. In the early days of the Peninsular history, nobility was lavishly bestowed on the Christian population, so that in Portugal this distinction was granted to a host of mercenary adventurers of different nations, who in the battle of Ourique, had fought against the Moors.* In Castile, the cultivators of the soil retained, to the latest period, their independence and their civil rights.

The nobles were altogether unmolested in their liberties; some of them were engaged in business and in trades, without any detriment to their titles. In Burgos, Osma, and the other ancient cities of Castile,† which had been founded for purposes different from those of French and German towns, the Knight's service was dependent on fortune, and not, as in other countries, on a particular station, or on the feudal tenure of lands. Every citizen, who possessed a certain amount of property, was bound to serve as *Caballero* (cavalier) or horseman in the king's army, and thereby acquired the same rights as the landed aristocracy. In some cities he received, by way of reward, certain immunities, such as exemption from taxation, &c. To the latest times, the nobles were, like inferior subjects, amenable to the civil jurisdiction. When the domination of the Spaniards spread more towards the south, the number of nobles appeared smaller in proportion to the extent of the population; for those Christians, who formerly had been subjects of the Moors, were now considered as ignoble, and therefore had first to acquire a title to nobility.

The number of Spanish nobles was, in consequence, increased to an enormous extent. Most of them, being poor and arrogant, brought on themselves the ridicule both of their countrymen and of the foreigner. The title of the nobles was inherited by all the descendants. The pride in those nominal distinctions is indicated by the name *Hidalgo*, (said to be derived from "Hyo d'Algo," *i. e.* the Son of Something). The term Caballero conveys an indefinite idea. It has ever been synonymous with "Gentleman," or a man raised above the plebeian multitude. It was an important prerogative of the

* They were totally defeated there by Alfonso I., King of Portugal, in 1139.—Tr.

† The cities of Castile were founded for the purpose of affording protection from the attacks of the Arabs. The citizens consisted of Nobles and Freemen; the crown being deficient in authority, the cities governed themselves like petty republics.

high-born, that they alone could be received into the rich military orders of knighthood. Marriages with plebeian wives did not affect the dignity or the privileges of gentle blood. By means of the conjunction *y,* which means *and,* sons used to add the maiden surname of their mother to the surname of the father. This custom shows, that according to popular opinion, nobility could be transmitted through the female line.

After the conquest of the Moorish provinces, the usages then introduced, partly coincided with those generally current, and partly, with those in force among the English nobles. At first, the Moors were expelled from the subjected territories, and the Caballeros were endowed with feudal benefices, on the same principles as in other parts of Europe. The poor labourers were not degraded to a state of servitude; still the feudal proprietor seems to have exercised full jurisdiction over his estate. This subject, however, is involved in obscurity; Spanish authors themselves are not clear upon it, nor upon the political rights of the nobility in the representation by the Cortes. It is not shown whether the rich noblemen (*ricos hombres*) possessed any privileges beyond those of the poorer *Hidalgos,* and whether they were regularly convoked to the Cortes. In one respect, the rich feudal aristocracy of Spain agreed with that of France and Germany. It exercised the revengeful right of feud to a great extent, and preferred wild freedom to the political power of a well-organised state. Until the days of Ferdinand the Catholic, the nobility frequently rose both against the crown and some special acts of government; but it never attained to the same independence as, at some periods, was acquired by the nobles of France and Germany.

In the reign of Ferdinand and Isabella, the nobility resolved itself into a more exclusive body. As early as the 11th century, the Christian states of Northern Spain had acquired such a superiority over the Moors, as to wrest from them considerable portions of their populous estates. The Moorish possessions became thereby reduced to a comparatively small district. For nearly three subsequent centuries, the national energy of the Spaniards appeared to be prostrated, and the tedious struggles with their enemies led to no material aggrandisement. Yet, within that period, the Mahometan population had gradually been pushed on to Granada; for in spite of all treaties, the

Christians sought to humiliate the Arabian inhabitants, whilst these avenged their defeats by the persecution and expulsion of the Christian rayahs. At the conquest of Granada, a portion of the original Moorish and Jewish population was suffered to remain in the country on condition of becoming converts. These remnants of the former inhabitants, though not debased as serfs, were held to be of inferior blood, and unfit to intermarry with persons of noble extraction.

Although the danger of defiling the old Christian blood could not always be avoided, the nobility guarded as much as possible against debasing their blood by matrimonial alliances with the new Christians. Until a recent period, government even indulged in intolerance to the new Christians by debarring them from civil and military offices, and from the grant of monopolies.

As in the provinces wrested from the Moors, a new nobility, constituted on the feudal system, was formed in the new world. America. On the conquest of an American territory, the lands were divided into fiefs, (*Comendadorias* or *encomiendas*), and allotted to the conquerors or the colonists. With the grant of such feudal benefices, were often connected the titles of Marquis and Count, (*Marques, Conde.*) The Aborigines of America were, at first, treated as slaves, but in the reign of Charles V., this servitude was abolished, as being incompatible with the laws of Spain. In the modern revolutions of America, the colonial nobility has been foremost in shaking off the supremacy of the mother country.

Aragon, forming a kingdom by itself, differed in its institutions from those of Castile. This state, it is true, had arisen from Aragon. the small principality of Navarre, but the greater part of it had formerly belonged to the Spanish border of Charlemagne's empire. There, the institutions of the Franks had a greater chance of success, because the land was a spoil of the conquerors, and had been divided at once into feudal allotments. The nobles were exceedingly numerous, and among them, the king was held as the first among his peers. The luckless freemen had gradually been reduced to servitude; in fact, the like condition obtained there as in France and in Germany, and only gave way, when the increasing influence of the cities mitigated the exclusiveness of the nobles; and again, it yielded when the peasantry, perhaps encouraged by the crown, reduced the oppressiveness of serfdom by a mutual compromise with the nobles. The right of feud was exercised by the latter for a very considerable time. It extended to the reign of Philip II., who by means of his arms as well as by his policy, crushed the liberties of the Aragonese, who had risen in insurrection against the tyranny of the Inquisition. The institutions of Castile, which were more liberal, appear to have re-acted on those of Aragon. There were nobles who engaged in trade, and even in the labours of the artizan. They might, for instance, deal in woollen cloth, without detriment to their dignity. The higher nobles had originally risen from the station of affluent land owners (*ricos hombres*). At a later period, when the crown conferred this title, no political or social immunities were implied by the grant. The so-called Grandees and Titulados of Castile lost much authority and power by the part they played under Charles V., as well as by numerous accessions to their orders. In the present age, these nobles are unfit to maintain such a position as is held by the English peerage; a position they might have acquired during the disturbances, which, in modern times, have convulsed their country.

In Italy, the distinctive claims of the nobles were based on the peculiar privileges of the cities, nearly all of which, after the fall of the empire, had secured to themselves some of the Italy. ancient municipal institutions, which continued together with the Roman civil law. After the lapse of a few centuries, these cities had become wealthy and influential republics.

In those parts of Italy where the Franks and Lombards had been dominant, the feudal nobility, at the fall of the Carlovingians, possessed the same unchecked liberties as in France. During the vigorous reigns of the German Emperors, the Othos, the authority of the sovereigns had gained the upper hand; but under Henry II., it yielded once more to the confusion arising from private feuds and civil conflicts, which, in France and Germany, had led to the dismemberment of the original monarchy. In Italy, the power of the great feudal lords had been broken by the policy of the Othos, and the land had been subdivided among such a numerous body of counts and barons, that the populous and ancient cities had no difficulty in asserting their independence, in vanquishing their noble neighbours, and in driving them to submission. So successful were the cities, that in the middle of the twelfth century, no more than four noble families remained in which the title to feudal chiefdom was preserved. We allude to the Margraves of Montferrat and to the families of Malaspina, Este, and Savoy.

The nobles, in all other parts of Northern Italy, were compelled to settle in towns, where they secured to themselves certain preferments to the highest administrative offices of their republics. Still they had to submit to elections, and were bound to furnish the heavy cavalry of the states. Nobility, founded on landed property, was thus merged into that rank of patricians which was held in low estimation by the aristocracy of France and of Germany, and which, in the Italian republics, descended from its height, and shared in all the vicissitudes of party strife. Only in a few of the numerous republics, the patrician nobles could permanently cope with the powerful and well-organised democracy. In many instances, these nobles lost both fortune and privileges. In Florence, for example, they were excluded from municipal offices and rights, as well as from the protection of judicial courts. In some states, as in Milan, they regained their footing after an expulsion and a defeat; in other parts of the land, they altogether ceased to exist. In the 13th century, when the Lombard republics were transformed into principalities, the ancient aristocracy was forced to share its rank with new families, which, in the struggle of factions, had risen from the low masses of the people. These promotions to civil honours were often reserved for the successful leaders of mercenary soldiers, (the *condottieri*) those roving adventurers of all grades and all nations, who did military duty for the effeminate Italians.

In Florence, after the ancient nobility had been suppressed, a new order of patricians sprang up from the several families of the ruling democrats, and, after having been invested with the highest magisterial powers for two generations, their authority became hereditary. This new nobility which exercised the utmost influence upon the progress of civilisation, includes the family of the Medici, who afterwards gave dukes to Tuscany. The Genoese nobles had a similar origin, but their aristocratic predecessors, (the families of Doria, Fieschi, Grimaldi, Spinola, &c.) though for some time excluded from the administration, had not to encounter the same political humiliation as in Florence. In later times, the patrician nobles who had risen from the lower grades of the people, (such were the Fregosi, Adorni, etc.) shared their authority with the members of the ancient aristocracy. Another portion of Italian nobles, distinguished for wealth and political eminence, nobles who extended their pretensions to remote ages, and whose descendants, afterwards, with much success, claimed the rank of princes,—we mean the patrician nobles of Venice,—had never been connected with the feudal system, but were the offspring of municipal dignitaries, who had held office for a series of many generations. This civic nobility exercised its exclusive rights very early. The great council, established in 1172, made elections to its own body, and treated the people's rights as empty forms. In 1291 and in 1300, laws were passed that no person should be admitted to the great council, whose paternal ancestors had not held similar office. In a few instances, this aristocracy reinforced itself by the admission of new members. The Venetian nobles, differed from other nobles in this respect, that their colleagues were permitted to trade as merchants; indeed, on the enterprise of those men depended the power and grandeur of the republic.

In the kingdom of Naples, the condition of the aristocracy remained altogether different from that of other states, though flourishing and mighty republics, such as Amalfi, etc., were ^{Naples.} also there established at the time of the Conquest by the Normans. The Norman family of Guiscard introduced into Naples a feudal constitution, (like that of France and Germany) which was respected by the Swabian emperors. When the Anjous conquered Naples, this constitution was more fully developed; the victorious army being mainly composed of Frenchmen of the Provence, where feudalism was flourishing. The territory afterwards changed proprietors, the old families being forced to yield to the French. As in France and Germany, turbulence and confusion arose in the kingdom of Naples, in consequence of the right of feud and the impotency of the crown. The peasants and even the inhabitants of cities were thrown into a state of dependence. The land was divided into greater or lesser fiefs, which often enjoyed actual independence, as was the case with the principality of Tarento. The government, on the whole deficient in authority, at last succumbed under the attacks of the French and Spaniards.

ON THE ESTABLISHMENT OF CHIVALRY.

The origin of chivalry has been traced back to the feudal system, Origin of Chivalry. and to the equestrian force maintained by the nobles of that system. It cannot however, be historically proved, at what time, and in which country chivalry was first established. Some writers have attempted to refer its introduction to the Crusades, but there are evidences of its actual establishment, with some peculiar characteristics, at the very commencement of the expeditions to the Holy Land. It has also been asserted that chivalry owed its origin to the French and Germans, but then we should be unable to account for the existence of that ancient specimen of Spanish chivalry, Don Roderigo de Bivar, commonly called the Cid, who commenced his career in the eleventh century. It is not likely that then, an active intercourse subsisted between secluded Castile and France,—much less between the former country and Germany. Some authors have ventured to assign the introduction of chivalry to the influence of Arabian education; but this assumption is contradicted by the fact that the followers of Eastern customs have ever objected to the courtesies of chivalry, and have withheld from the individual warrior that independence of action, for which such ample provision was made by the institution of knighthood. It is true the Spanish Moors adopted various chivalric forms, and their nobles, armed in European fashion, were, even by their enemies, designated as knights; but such coincidences, in point of warfare and in some matters of a social nature, were due to the frequent contact of the Moors with the Christian inhabitants of Spain.

We have observed that the political circumstances, which promoted the formation of a feudal aristocracy, or gave ascendancy Causes of its general adoption. to the heavy-armed horsemen, were analogous among nearly all nations of the German race. Besides political, there were yet other causes, which operated in the establishment of chivalry among these nations. All of them appeared actuated by a certain religious zeal, which stimulated them to wage war against infidels, and to propagate Christianity by the force of arms. Among the Franks, this bigotry was displayed in the reign of Charles Martel, and especially during the reign of Charlemagne. It aroused the Germans to engage in the expeditions against the Wends, Sclavonians, and Lithuanians; it led the Spaniards to oppose the Moors, and it induced the Christians generally to warlike enterprises in the East.

A peculiar feature in the German character, known even to Tacitus, was the deference shewn to the fair sex. In the German Influence of the Fair Sex. states, formed from the ruins of the Roman empire, the influence of woman on government as well as on national rights and usages, is sufficiently obvious, though the mutual relations of both sexes cannot be clearly determined. Taking a general view of circumstances, common to all the nations of German origin, we are induced to think that chivalry was more the result of ancient usages than of modern institutions. As regards England and Scandinavia, chivalry was merely transplanted thither from other countries. In England, it was introduced by the Norman Conqueror, and in Denmark and Sweden, through intercourse with foreign nations. Chivalry spread with great rapidity in all these countries, because the national habits were adapted to its institutions.

Those countries which produced an early independent literature, were most favorable to the development of chivalry. The Literature of Languedoc. south of France occupies, in this respect, the first place. The lyrical poetry of the southern poets, the Troubadours, bears evidence as to the refinement (Cortesia) of the nobility. This courtesy was one of the leading features of chivalry, and engaged the poets in occasionally stiff and formal *Tensons,** *Pastorals, Lays, &c.* Generosity, gallantry, justice, and religious demeanour are there represented as the foundation of chivalric honour. These requisites are coupled with the unrestrained propensities of the warrior, who indulges to the fullest extent in the right of feud, and is as clamorous for his independence as for his reputation. A strange mixture of knightly virtue with the fierceness of an incessantly embroiled aristocracy, is to be found in the poems called *Sirventes.†* Replete with threats and animosity, they dwell, with passionate vehemence, on war and combat; but, on the other hand, these violent feelings seem to give

* The Tenson (in Provençal Tensos or Contenciôs) contained the versified debates of two rival poets. When more than two were engaged in the poetical contest, the poem was entitled " *Torneimens*," (Tournament.)—Tr.

† Sirventes was the term applied to political poems of praise or blame. This class of poetry was written in the *service* and under the auspices of some patron lord, hence its name.—Tr.

way to the dictates of the church and of the ladies, as well as to the obligations of justice and of generosity.

Instead of a series of lyrical poetry, peculiar to the south of France, the northern French have a long array of romances and *Literature of the North of France.* historical memoirs of the thirteenth, fourteenth, and fifteenth centuries. These works afford an insight into the minutest details of chivalry. The romances are of sufficient authority to yield an idea of current manners and customs. A considerable amount of information is to be derived from the chronicles and histories, composed by cotemporary authors, who, in a plain, unpretending style, give a faithful representation of the general character of their times. To this class of works belong the History of St. Louis, by Joinville, Froissart's Chronicles, (written during the wars between the French and Edward III., King of England), and the biographies of Marshal Boucicault and of Bertrand Du Guesclin, which were once frequently reprinted, and have been republished in the valuable collection of Buchon. Also, Brantôme, of the sixteenth century, may be added to this list. Although that writer did not live within the period of the middle ages, the forms of knighthood, in his time, were still in high estimation and in lively remembrance. Finally, we mention the best work on chivalry, composed by a Frenchman shortly before the revolution. It bears the title, " Mémoires sur l'Ancienne Chevalerie, par M. de la Curne de Sainte Palaye."

Chivalry varied in extent, like the feudal system, with which it was intimately connected. In those countries, where the *Chivalry in different Countries.* aristocracy was numerically limited, the admission to the dignity of knighthood was similarly restricted. The largest number of knights was to be found in England and in Castile; the smallest number in France and in Aragon. The latter province being part of Charlemagne's Spanish boundary, its aristocratic institutions accorded most with those of France and Germany. In Castile, promotion to knighthood was not limited to birth alone; it was dependent also on the wealth of the citizen; in Aragon, however, birth alone determined the admission to the honours of chivalry. In England, since the reign of Henry III., any commoner could be made a knight; the power of conferring this dignity being vested in the crown.

In France, where the feudal system was more fully developed than elsewhere, men of common origin were altogether excluded from the rank of knighthood. The code of St. Louis expressly says: " If any man whose father is a plebeian be made a knight, the king or the baron in whose estate he is domiciled, may order that the spurs of such a pretender be struck off on a dunghill." In Germany the accolade granted by the emperor raised a man at once to the station of nobility. But in the reign of Sigismund, knights, like the patricians of municipal towns, were no longer held equal to nobles. In Italy, patrician families were admitted to the honour of knighthood, yet, on acquiring this title, they enjoyed no special privileges among the independent republican citizens.

Chivalry, considered from a social and military point of view, afforded to the feudal nobles of all countries, the advantage of placing them on an equal footing with each other. Indigent knights, of inferior descent, possessed, in times of war, certain privileges, which were denied to those nobles who had not been admitted to the honours of knighthood. Young men who had been knighted, met, in times of war, with no impediment in their promotion, and could even attain to the highest command. Boucicault, for example, became Marshal of France at the age of twenty-five, and La Trimouille, a French general under Charles VII., was appointed lieutenant-general of the realm at the age of twenty-eight, after having gained a decisive battle in Brittany.

The military achievements of chivalry are, in a great measure, due to the strict discipline and rigid forms which mark the early training of the tyro. The following description will throw *The training of young Noblemen.* some light on the education of young knights. The boy, in his seventh year, was removed from his home, or at least, from the supervision of females, and entered the service of some superior or inferior nobleman. There, he was chiefly occupied with bodily exercises of a severe character. His services consisted in attendance upon his master, or the family, and he was but little distinguished from the domestics of the household. This method of training young noblemen prevailed in France and many other countries as late as the 16th, and was only gradually discontinued at the end of the 17th century. Between the ages of fourteen and seventeen, the tyro was

Squire.
made squire (*escuyer, escudero, esquire*). This promotion was distinguished by a religious solemnity. The young man after being conducted to the altar, either by his parents, or by their representatives, who carried lighted wax-tapers,—the priest blessed a sword that had been placed on the altar, and then girded the young nobleman with it. He was then exercised in the use of arms, etc. In reference to these exercises, it is stated in the biography of Boucicault,

Boucicault's Muscular Exercise.
that he himself, when fully armed, attempted to leap upon a charger, that he also ran a great distance on foot, so as to habituate himself to keep his breath. He then with his axe or mace, struck powerful blows at thick logs of wood, or blocks of stone. Being anxious to inure himself to the weight of his armour, and to strengthen his hands and arms, he took leaps completely equipped, with the exception of his helmet; he mounted his horse fully armed and without stirrups, and also danced about in a hauberk of chain-mail; he vaulted on the shoulders of a tall man, who sat on a high horse, with no other help than that of seizing the man by his sleeves. Resting one hand on the pommel of the saddle, and the other on the ears of a high charger, he leaped over it without losing his hold. If two walls were close together, he skilfully and fearlessly climbed up, with no other assistance than the strength of his arms and legs. He was accustomed to climb up the inner side of a ladder, when leaning against a wall, merely by raising his hands from one step to another, without touching the ladder with his feet. Divesting himself of his hauberk, he used only one hand in raising himself from one step to another. With other squires, he practised the art of darting the lance, or occupied himself with other military exercises.

In a like manner, the King of France, Henry IV., was wont to prepare himself for combat in heavy armour, as we learn from the memoirs of Sully. The considerable weight of offensive and defensive arms naturally demanded great muscular strength and agility, which could only be acquired by arduous exercise. The description given above renders it evident that a lad of a delicate constitution must have sunk under such severe trials of strength.

Duties of the Squire.
Early acquaintance with the nature and treatment of horses was essential to mounted noblemen. The young squire had therefore to attend at the stables, where he received practical hints from his seniors. He was also obliged to perform inferior military service, to become habituated to the discipline of battle. Thus, for instance, it was his duty at midnight, to patrol castles. The squires ordinarily learnt the use of defensive arms by waiting on their lords in the camp and at tournaments. Much practice and great exactness were required in putting on the armour, so as to secure the safety and success of the combatants. Particular skill was even requisite in joining the clasps of the armour and in attaching the visor. Negligence in fixing the latter was the alleged cause of the death of Henry II., King of France. The squire attended to the habiliments of his lord, in the last moments of emergency, when the approach of the enemy imposed upon the knight the necessity of being fully equipped.

When engaged on an expedition, the knight rode on a light horse, unarmed, or protected only by a cuirass. Other portions of the armour, together with a stronger charger, were brought up immediately before the combat took place, or when any danger was imminent.

During the battle, the squires were kept apart from the knights. The latter were drawn up in an extensive line, and, their horses, being put to full speed, they dashed with their lances against their opponents. The squires formed a second line. Each of them was obliged to watch the movements of his master, assist him in cases of emergency, and supply him with fresh weapons. When the battle was over, the squires were charged with the custody of the prisoners. In an encounter with a hostile knight, the squire was enjoined to observe the defensive. In the days of Francis I., King of France, this mode of combat was still in fashion. It is related by Brantôme, that when the king's squire of honour, at Pavia, saw his royal master in danger, he parried off the blows levelled at him, and in this defence, met with his death.

This system gave way to attacks of cavalry in columns or squadrons, which, among the Germans and Spaniards, were first made under Charles V., who probably owed to them his superiority over the French. The same system was adopted in France during the war with the Huguenots. The ancient mode of placing the squire in the rear, gave rise to the designation of Poursuivants (*i. e.*, those who follow). This word was adopted by the Germans in the corrupt form of "Perseveranten."

Respecting outward signs of rank, the squires were permitted to wear
Restrictions in Dress. ornaments of silver, but not of gold; the most precious metal being exclusively reserved for the knights. In like manner, the squires were only allowed to clothe themselves in garments of ordinary silks and furs. Scarlet dresses were forbidden to them. Their defensive armour in war and at tournaments was of a lighter and inferior description, so that they could not well infringe upon the prohibition of fighting with heavy-armed knights.

The social accomplishments of young noblemen were, like their
Subordinate Position of Young Nobles. military training, of an exclusive character, and the results of gradually acquired habits. The squires, when initiated in their duties, held a menial position. Services, in the estimation of the Romans, derogatory to freemen, were not considered incompatible with the honour of the German nobility, even at the earliest ages. The Merovingians and other kings of German origin surrounded themselves with a suite of nobles, who, in addition to their public functions, were obliged to perform personal service. At a later period, this fashion was imitated by rich feudal lords, in relation to squires. These served at the banquet as carvers, offered the water for ablution, poured out wine, etc. Thus they came in constant contact with knights, and obtained a practical acquaintance with the manners of society, though they were not permitted to join in conversation.

Joinville, in his *Histoire de St. Louis,* has shewn that such services were, by no means, derogatory. He himself, as squire, at the table of Louis IX., had to wait upon the king of Navarre. At the same banquet, the king was served by his own brother, the Count of Artois, and the young Count of Soissons. Froissart, also, in extolling the magnificence and chivalric bearing of the Count de Foix, observes that this nobleman was usually served at table by his own son. At the courts of the rich feudal nobility, such customs tended to increase the number of squires. In battle, numerous retainers of this class were indispensable, for the purpose of loading the horses, assisting the knights in putting on their armour, carrying the arms, and performing personal services. The body-squire, or squire of honour (*escuyer du corps* or *d'honneur*), held the first rank among them. He carried the banner of his lord, followed him closely, and acted as confidential servant.

When a young nobleman had attained his twenty-first year, his education was completed, and he was considered as of age. Investiture of the Squire. He was now invested with his armour, and entitled to engage in combat, from which, hitherto, he had been debarred; in fact, he now became eligible to the rank of knighthood. Among the Spaniards, who followed the precedence of the Visigoths, majority and admission to knighthood were attained at the age of twenty. The Cid received the accolade even before he had reached these years, he having then already given proofs of his valour, both in single combat and in a victory over the Moors.

The introduction to knighthood consisted of a ceremony which varied in detail. The best original account of the solemnities peculiar to such an occasion is given in the old French poem, "Hugh of Tiberias," (*Hue de Tabarie*). It was composed about the thirteenth century, and furnishes a plain and faithful description of the rites observed on the admission to the dignity of knighthood, as well as of the symbolical signification of such a ceremony. The following outline of the poem will throw some light on The Inauguration symbolically interpreted. the forms and the allegorical meaning of the accolade.

Hugh, Prince of Tiberias, is made prisoner in a battle with Saladin. The sultan is willing to let the captive knight, on parole, return to his native land, where he is to collect his ransom within the term of three years. Hugh, on the point of leaving, is solicited by the sultan to confer on him the dignity of knighthood. Hugh at first, objects, on the plea of Saladin being an infidel; at last, however, he yields, and goes through the performance of the several rites. He dresses the sultan's hair and beard, then takes him to a bath, saying, that he must leave his bath unpolluted by depravity, and free from sin, like a child that is raised from the baptismal font; henceforth, he must practise honesty, courtesy, and benevolence, and earn the regard of all men. He then lays him on a bed, observing: " This is a symbol of the bed of rest in paradise, which is attainable by chivalric demeanour, and denied to the unrighteous." The sultan having risen, Hugh dresses him in white linen, with the injunction: " This is a sign of the cleanliness in which you have to keep your body during this life, if you wish to be received by God." He then invests the Sultan with a scarlet cloak, and says: " This colour represents blood, which you must at all times be ready to shed in the service of God, and in defence of the church." Then putting the shoes on the Sultan's feet, he adds: "This black covering of the feet must ever remind you of death, and of the earth from which you have been fashioned, and unto which you will return. Cherish no pride: it is unbecoming in a knight, but adhere to simplicity and singleness of purpose." The Sultan having risen, Hugh girds him with a white cincture, and repeating the injunction about external cleanliness, adds, that his body must remain in a state of virgin purity, free from every pollution and licence; the latter he must despise and abhor. He then fastens the gilded spurs on the feet of the Sultan, admonishing him with respect to the service of God, and the performance of chivalric duties, to be as swift and spirited as the charger in the race when pressed by the spurs. In handing him the two-edged sword, he offers the following explanation: "The one edge is intended for your self-defence; the other must serve to protect the poor from being trodden down by the rich, and you are bound to support the weak, when the powerful seek to illtreat them." The act of girding the sword being completed, the knight covers the head of the Sultan with a white cap, saying: "As this head-dress, thy soul shall be clean and spotless, unaffected by the infatuation of the flesh, it must surrender unto God on the day of judgment, in order that it may enter paradise." The final ceremony, the accolade, is withheld by the knight, who states that as a prisoner he is not allowed to confer it, but that it is intended to impress the new knight with a grateful remembrance of him who has raised him to this dignity. At last he charges the Sultan with the knightly duties of acting with justice, courtesy, and piety, and also of being charitable to the poor.

These inaugural rites were not at all times alike. Ordinarily the ceremony took place in a church after the young nobleman Inauguration. had duly prepared himself by fasting, confessing, and taking the sacrament. He approached the altar in plain attire, the sword, attached to a scarf, being suspended from his shoulder. After presenting the sword to the priest, who blessed it, he knelt down. On some occasions the candidate was interrogated why he desired to join the order, and he was reminded, that the inactive enjoyment of honours was as objectionable in the chivalric order as in the sacerdotal calling. Then the young nobleman was invested with the whole suit of armour. On some occasions this service was partly rendered by ladies. When fully armed he was dubbed. The officiating knight struck him thrice on the shoulder or the neck with the flat side of the sword, or gave him a blow on the face with the palm of his hand. French writers relate, that knights in performing the ceremony of the accolade, made use of some such words as the following: "In the name of St. Michael, and St. George, I nominate thee, etc."; some used to add the admonition; "Be brave, bold, and loyal." Occasionally the new knight was warned not to submit to another dubbing. The newly installed knight had also to take a solemn oath; a custom which relaxed in stringency during the decline of the middle ages. Finally, the new knight, fully equipped and furnished with helmet and shield, showed himself on horseback to the assembled people.

The only ceremony indispensable in conferring the dignity of knighthood, consisted in the accolade (la colée). By this The accolade simple process many warriors were knighted before or during war. after battle. Those promoted before battle, were generally drawn up in the first line, so as to give them a chance of displaying their prowess. It is related by Froissart, that Dionysius, King of Portugal, during a battle with the Castilians summoned those of his army who wished to be knighted, and promised he would confer that honour upon them in the name of God and St. George. It appears that sixty knights were created on that occasion. The king felt great satisfaction in placing them in the foremost line, and addressed them thus: "Dear Sirs, chivalry is so exalted, that it repudiates all reproach. A knight must have a spotless character, and manifest no meanness or cowardice; he must be proud and bold as a lion when he sees his enemies. I now desire you to show your bravery in the right place, and I therefore place you in the front of the ranks: acquit yourselves in such a manner that we and you may derive honour from your conduct, lest your spurs would be ill-bestowed."

The same author in his account of the battle of Crecy, speaks of the high estimation in which the accolade was held. He says, that when Edward III. was informed that his son, the Black Prince, was surrounded by the enemy and in imminent peril, he enquired: "Is he dead or fallen from his horse, or so grievously wounded that he cannot defend himself?" The messenger answered, that the prince was alive, but exposed to danger. The king then said, "Tell those who have sent you, that so long as my son lives, they shall never again apply to me for aid, for I desire them to let him gain his spurs. If it please God, I trust, this day will prove auspicious to my son, and yield him honour." The same chronicler, in describing a battle between the Portuguese and Spaniards, states that some Frenchmen in the Castilian camp, were knighted after a reconnaissance, in which they had an encounter with the Portuguese army. The number of knights thus created was often very great. In 1412, at the siege of Bourges, more than 500 men were at once made knights. Francis I., after having fought in the battle of Marignano, was knighted by Bayard. This custom was not restricted to battles on land; among the English at least, it seems to have been a frequent occurrence, that those who distinguished themselves in sea-fights, were rewarded with promotion to knighthood. According to Froissart, this was done when the fleet attacked the city of Cayant. In the reign of Elizabeth, it was usual for the commander of every large vessel to be knighted if he had, in any way, distinguished himself. In many instances, promotion to knighthood took place before the battle; and often the claims of the candidate were previously examined by heralds. Also in times of peace, there were occasions when the nobles were made knights in large numbers without going through the above-mentioned ceremonies. Promotions used to take place during some festivals of the church, as at Whitsuntide; at the coronation and nuptials of sovereigns, on occasions of the births of princes, on conferring and receiving grants of extensive fiefs, etc. The honours of knighthood used also to be awarded after tournaments: mostly, however, these sports succeeded the nomination of knights who there found a favourable opportunity of displaying their dexterity in the use of arms.

The ceremony of investing young men with arms was antecedent *Antiquity of investiture.* to the existence of feudal nobility and to chivalry itself. We find notices of such inaugural rites in the *Germania* of Tacitus, and in the accounts which have come down to us from the days of the Carlovingians. Charlemagne handed the sword to his son Louis at a grand meeting of the people; and, with equal publicity, Louis the Pious girded his son Charles with the sword. In England, before the Norman conquest, the young Saxon nobles were admitted to the exercise of their privileges by inaugural forms, which there partook of a religious character.

A blow on the face was not peculiar to the nomination of knights, but characterised various occasions of inauguration. *Instances of Dubbing.* Even mechanics on being admitted as members of trade corporations were received by a blow on the face. The following remarkable case of dubbing, mentioned by Grimm,* deserves to be noticed. The Dukes of Carinthia, until the fifteenth century, took possession of their land and subjects by a symbolical ceremony: before receiving homage, the duke, attended by the nobles of the land, presented himself with gifts, before a free peasant, who was seated on the ducal throne. After some questions and answers, the gifts were offered to the peasant, who, exhorting the duke to adhere to justice, descended from the throne and gave him a blow on the face. The duke was thereby symbolically installed in his dominion; the blow, in this case, as in that of admitting to the honours of knighthood, was intended to direct the attention of the new dignitary to those who had figuratively charged him with the duties of his high rank.

As regards external distinctions, knights alone were allowed to appear in costly attire, at tournaments and at court; moreover, they were honoured by the respective titles of *Herr, Messire,* *Outward distinction of knights.* *Don, Sir,* while those nobles who had not yet attained this title had only a right to the designation of *Junker, Damoisel, i. e.,* young lord. The latter were not allowed to attach their seals to judicial documents, but had to borrow them from their relations or superiors. If the honour of knighthood was conferred before the young cavalier had reached his twenty-first year, he was treated as being of age.

The knights among themselves enjoyed equality of social and military rank. The difference between a common knight *Equality.* (*Chevalier Bachelier*) and a Banneret merely consisted in this, that the wealthier nobles possessed the latter title, if they could furnish, at their own expense, a number of armed men. The indigent knight was not lowered in rank by becoming the retainer of another knight. The bannerets, as a mark of distinction, had a pennon or square banner attached to their lances, whilst the common knights

* Rechtsalterthümer, p. 253.

only carried pennoncelles or small banners, the sides of which were indented and terminated in two points. The bannerets used also to receive a larger share of booty and of the gifts bestowed on them, when employed in ambassadorial missions, as well as at the celebration of certain festivities.

Chivalry offers even a religious aspect. The inaugural observances, explained in the poem " *Hue de Tabarie*," bear evidence to the importance of religious qualifications, and the duty of protecting the church as a matter of personal honour. It is needless to expatiate on the fact, that religion and the military spirit of the age aided each other in making the subjection and conversion of infidels, the holy cause of christian states. A strict compliance with the outward forms of religion was, on all sides, enforced by physical means. In the poem just referred to, the knight is expected to exemplify his piety by fasting on Fridays, going to hear mass every day, and by giving alms. The knight attending mass is entitled to appear in his suit of armour, and to cut down any one who should venture to revile the sacrament. It is related in an ancient chronicle, (quoted in Du Cange's Glossary, under the word *Evangelium*), that the knights in the suite of the emperor Charles IV., stood with swords, drawn and raised, during the time the gospel was read; intimating thereby their readiness to defend their faith with the point of the sword. Such religious demonstrations of chivalry grew into fashion, and were undoubtedly promoted by the enterprises of the crusaders. A strange specimen of knightly piety is afforded by Stephen Vignolles, commonly called Lahire, who in 1427, was marching against the English. On approaching the camp of the enemy, he applied to a chaplain for absolution of his sins; being desired to confess, Lahire replied that he had no time to do so, as he must without delay attack the enemy, and that his conduct had only been such, as that of warriors generally is. The chaplain then gave him absolution, and Lahire with folded hands offered up the following prayer: " God I pray thee that this day thou mayest do for Lahire, what thou desirest Lahire should do for thee, if he were God, and thou Lahire !"

Religious aspect of Chivalry.

Outward devotion, and gallantry to the fair sex, were peculiar to the ancient Germans, and were inherited by the nobility of the middle ages. Young men were taught, that love to

The Fair Sex.

God, and love to the ladies, were almost of the same significance. The duty of protecting the weak, which Hugh of Tiberias symbolically connects with the edge of the sword, excited enthusiasm when ladies became the objects of protection. The author of that *Fabliau* enjoins knights never to refuse their aid to a lady, and to offer their assistance to the best of their abilities, if they be desirous to earn praise and renown. Courtesy, based upon respect to the fair sex, evidently had considerable effect upon mediæval manners. Ladies being present at the entertainments of the court, checked the coarseness of a warlike and tyrannical aristocracy; they joined the knights at their banquets, and ate with them out of the same plates; they attended the tournaments and assisted in the distribution of prizes, as well as in unharnessing the armed knights. The latter, on the other hand, fought in honour of the beauty of their ladies, and bore their devices and colours.

The influence of courtesy, even on the field of battle, has been described by Froissart, who in his chronicle, relates the following anecdotes: A French knight, named Bonnelance, was once asked by some ladies in Montferrand to engage in a daring adventure against the English. Amongst those ladies was one he loved, and who had expressed a wish to get sight of an Englishman. Bonnelance replied, if I succeed in capturing some of the enemy, I will bring them to you. Soon afterwards he placed some Englishmen before that lady, and said to her, I will leave them with you till they pay for their board. The offer, observes the chronicler, afforded the ladies much merriment, and made them thankful to the knight. At another time, a Frenchman, whilst engaged in a reconnaissance, rode to the wall of the fortress and called up to the sentry, " Who is your captain? Tell him that knight Languerant challenges him. Your captain is a good and valiant knight, for his lady's sake he will not give me a refusal. Should he reject my challenge, he will be dishonoured, and I will everywhere expose his disgrace." The Englishman, who was summoned to fight in honour of his lady, at once complied, and after a severe struggle he triumphed over the Frenchman, who lost his life in the encounter. The following anecdote is still more striking. At the siege of Cherbourg the combat became very fierce, when a Frenchman desired to fight with the most ardent of English

Courtesy displayed in War.

lovers. The challenge was accepted, and the *mêlée* ceased for a while. During the single combat, one of the champions fell a victim to his love, and then the general fight was resumed with renewed bitterness. God and Love were in those days regarded as equivalent terms; Froissart intimates that with the help of God and of Love, he had undertaken to make a collection of erotic songs. In like manner Boccacio thanks God and Love for aiding him in the composition of his Decameron.

Even legislation bore traces of these gallant sentiments; James II. of Aragon decreed as follows : " We desire that any one travelling with a lady shall proceed freely and unmolestedly, unless he be guilty of murder." It must not be supposed that this deference to ladies was of an ideal and platonic nature. The French and German poetical works of that age betray a strong tendency to sensuality. The over-refinement of Provençal poetry, and the courts of love, which have been put forth as proofs of exalted reverence to the fair sex, were mere pastimes for idlers, and seem to have been akin to the casuistry of contemporary scholastics.

This courtesy was a duty, both in war and in social intercourse. _{Generosity to enemies.} To offend against it, and behave ungenerously towards a vanquished foe was as abhorrent as faithlessness and treachery. Prisoners were liberated by paying a ransom to the amount of one year's revenue, or by pledging their word, that on returning to their homes, they would collect the sum required for their ransom. " After the battle of Poitiers," says Froissart, " each English and Gascon knight ordered his prisoner, whether knight or squire, to state, upon his honour, what amount of ransom he could conveniently pay. The sum having been named, the prisoner was made debtor for that amount. Some of the victorious party even declared that they would not injure any knight or squire, by depriving him of the means necessary for the support of his dignity. After that battle, the Black Prince showed the utmost deference to the captive king. In consideration of the rank of the prisoner, he would not sit with him at the same table, and he comforted him by saying : ' It appears to me you have much cause to be satisfied, though the battle did not terminate according to your wishes, for you have this day earned a high reputation for valour and you have excelled your best champions. Every one of our army who witnessed the exertions of the two

parties has conscientiously acknowledged this, and awards you the prize and the wreath of glory.' " Another still more brilliant instance of generosity is, by the same author, related of Edward III. This king, in single combat, captured a French knight, who had attacked Calais during an armistice. He sat down at table with his prisoner, reproved him slightly, and then added, that he had never encountered a knight so well skilled in fighting, and that he must, in fairness, assign to him the prize of honour, in preference to all the paladins of his court. The king then took off his head-gear, ornamented with pearls, and placed it on the head of the knight, saying : " Sir Eustache, I give you this ornament, you being the best of champions, and I request you to wear it this year, for my sake ; I know that you are disposed to mirth and love, and also fond of the society of ladies ; state therefore everywhere, that I have presented you with this gift. You are dismissed from custody ; to-morrow, you may depart." Such courtesy seems to have mitigated the bitterness even of civil war. An Italian chronicler of the thirteenth century, in describing the fall of the tyrant Eccelin,* censures the soldier who wounded this chief of the Ghibelins after he had been taken prisoner. " That warrior," he says, " merited no praise ; he deserved the disgrace of infamy, for it is as great an iniquity to offend or strike a captive nobleman or commoner, as to mutilate a corpse with a sword."

Politeness, generous contempt of money, and the most liberal hospitality, became the fashion of nobles in all countries. _{Mutual attentions.} Foreign knights were not only regaled at every court, but generally received some gifts in addition. The Black Prince, according to Froissart, gave 500 marks to a knight who had distinguished himself at the battle of Poitiers. The knight immediately distributed the money among the squires of his corps, and the Prince, hearing of this, presented 600 marks to the same knight. Of the facility in collecting the required ransom, the following anecdote affords an illustration. Bertrand du Guesclin, on being desired by the Black Prince to fix the fee of his release, _{Ransom.} offered an exorbitant sum, stating : " The kings of France

* Eccelin, or Ezzelino da Romano, born in 1194, at the castle of Onara, in Treviso, was one of the most ambitious and ferocious leaders of party in Italy. His perseverance in exterminating the noblest families of Padua and Verona was fully in keeping with the self-assumed title, " the Scourge of God."—Tr.

and of Castile are my friends, they will not prove faithless. In Brittany, I know an hundred knights who will sell their estates to liberate me. Besides, there is not a woman in France that plies her spindle who would not work for the sake of contributing towards my ransom." Applications of indigent knights for gifts of money, which now would be considered begging, were then not regarded as dishonourable. The following story, which is related by Joinville, bears out this remark : a poor knight was kneeling before the Count of Champagne, surnamed the Liberal, and solicited a gift as a dower for his two daughters. A rich citizen, wishing to rid the Count of these importunities, told the petitioner, his lord had already distributed such large sums, that nothing was left to him. The count thereupon exclaimed : " Citizen, thou liest in saying, I have nothing left to give away ; thou art yet my property. Sir Knight, I make you a present of this bondman." The poor knight at once seized the citizen by his dress, and assured him that he would not let him go, unless he paid his ransom. The citizen then gave him the sum of 500 livres. The dismissal of prisoners on their word of honour was justified by that sense of honour which constituted a fundamental principle of chivalry. Traitors forfeited their claims to knighthood and the chances of being protected by those, to whom their faithlessness had been of advantage.

In the romances of the Cid, it is related, that King Sancho was warned by an enemy to guard against a suspicious nobleman, *Treachery and its punishment.* who had made his way into the royal camp. The king, heedless of the warning, was murdered by that nobleman. The inhabitants of Zamora, though benefitted by that murder, refused all intercourse with the assassin. The chief nobles dressed in mourning, and offered to prove the guiltlessness of their fellow-citizens, in an ordeal of single combat. The word of a knight was given and generally received as an unexceptionable pledge. On the other hand, knights were apt to adopt expedients which do not accord with our notions of fairness. The Cid, desirous to borrow money of some Jews, pledged with them two heavy chests, which, he pretended, were filled with silver, but in reality were laden with stones. The money-lenders were obliged to promise that the chests should not be opened before payment was due. At the stipulated time, he honestly redeemed his pledges.

Chivalry extended its attention to the duties of friendship. It has already been remarked, that the bestowal of the accolade *Brotherhood in arms.* favoured such relations of intimacy. The same act also tended to establish fraternities of arms, which were vowed for life or for some specific enterprise. On occasions of such mutual adoption, knights either took the sacrament, or each opened a vein, and they intermixed their blood, or they exchanged weapons. Brothers in arms shared friend and foe with each other. They could only be allowed to fight with each other, if they belonged to two nations which were engaged in war. If one of them became a prisoner of war, the other was bound to procure the ransom. Brotherhood in arms superseded the duties of courtesy, so that a knight thus pledged could refuse the protection claimed by a lady.

Faithlessness, treachery, and cowardly flight, like other delinquencies of a base character, were visited by the forfeiture *Degradation of knights.* of knighthood. The dignity of knighthood, which was conferred by a particular solemnity, was also solemnly withdrawn. The condemned knight was led to a scaffold, on which his sword, lance, and armour, were broken and trodden under foot. His shield, with its escutcheon defaced, and turned upside down, was tied to a horse's tail, and dragged through the mire. A priest read the funeral service over him, and recited the 109th Psalm, which contains imprecations against traitors. Heralds at arms thrice called the name of the disgraced knight, and each time the squire responded that this knight was now degraded. A squire then poured hot water upon his head to remove the sanctity of the accolade. Finally, the degraded knight, with a rope fastened under his arm-pits, was pulled down from the scaffold, covered with a shroud, and dragged on a hurdle to church, where the funeral rites were performed over him. Such punishments fell to the lot of many Knight Templars in the reign of Philip the Fair. In some parts of Germany, a degraded knight was forced to wear boots without spurs, and bestride a horse, unshod and unsaddled, which he had to lead by a bridle of osier bark. For minor offences, as for retreating, or losing a battle, the table-cloth of the knight who sat down with others to a meal, was cut to pieces, and a loaf of bread was laid down before him on the wrong side. Such punishments were often publicly inflicted by the herald at arms, but did not deprive the knight of his rank.

Before closing this subject, we have to advert to a few customs and usages incidental to the outward forms of chivalry.

Eccentricities. Knights who were engaged in military adventures for the sake of courtesy, or in real warfare, wore in some parts of their armour small chains, as tokens of their engagements. Such tokens, which had been fastened by the hands of ladies, amidst certain religious rites, were worn until the particular vow was fulfilled. Of a more trying nature were those self-imposed restrictions, which occasionally marked the ardour of knightly combatants. Du Guesclin, for example, swore, at the siege of Moncontour, to abstain from meat and to wear the same apparel, till the place should be taken. In the first campaign of Edward III., some English knights wore covers over one of their eyes. They had vowed to their ladies that they would refrain from looking at them with both eyes, unless they gained distinction in the field of battle. This show became altogether puerile in the ostentatious and extravagant vow of "the peacock"* or "the pheasant." Such a vow, attended by fanciful pageantry, was occasioned by Philip of Burgundy, in 1543. While a banquet was being held, a grand procession entered, showing the perilous state of religion after the conquest of Constantinople. A lady, who personated Religion, recited a poem in which she sought to excite the fanaticism of the assembled knights. Then entered the king-at-arms of the Golden Fleece, followed by a long train of knights. He carried a pheasant, adorned with a golden necklace, which was set with pearls and diamonds. The bird was offered to the duke, who thereupon made a vow to engage in a crusade. The oath began as follows: "I vow unto God, unto the Holy Virgin, and also unto the Ladies, and unto the Pheasant, etc." The formula was then repeated by the other knights, amidst various demonstrations of enthusiasm. This performance led to no practical result, as the crusade was only to be set on foot under certain conditions, which did not come to pass.

Other solemnities and usages of chivalry will be described hereafter, in our essay on tournaments.

* Grimm, (Rechtsalterthümer, p. 901), is inclined to trace this vow to the period of the Frankish empire. "A Peacock Feast," copied from a brass plate in the Church of St. Margaret, Kings's Lynn, is depicted in Warner's *Antiquitates Culinariæ.*—TR.

ON MEDIÆVAL ARMOUR.

Warlike barbarians, owing to their habits and their mode of living, place great value upon their weapons; hence the manufacture of arms is one of the first industrial pursuits at the dawn of civilisation. For this reason, we discover among the ancient Germans, some amount of skill in the working of iron. In the ancient Scandinavian sagas, the smith who made swords, knives, and rings, is placed in the foremost rank, by the side of the singer, who attended royalty. The armourer holding a prominent position is mentioned in the legends which commemorate popular heroes. A striking instance of this is given in the Wilkinga saga, in the person of Wieland, the smith. Tacitus informs us, that the swords and spears of the Germans, being clumsy and unwieldy, were ill-calculated to resist the skilfully-wrought and efficient arms of the Roman legions. After the reigns of the Antonines, the Germans continually overran the Roman empire, and gradually learnt to use the defensive armour of their more civilised opponents. At the same time, they became familiar with the process of tempering steel, and of applying the same in their national arms. Even the wildest of the German tribes, the Vandals, whose success and dominion in Gaul, Spain, and Africa, were marked by devastation, surpassed the Italians, after the overthrow of the empire, in the manufacture of weapons. In their forges, they wrought damaskeened blades, which were hard enough to cut iron.

Before any other industrial productions began to circulate in the western dominions, the manufacture of arms had already risen to some importance. In addition to fur, arms seem to have formed the principal articles of commerce, and so late as the end of the twelfth century, were taken in exchange of Indian goods from the Saracens. The extent of the traffic is attested by many laws, which, prohibiting the sale of arms, were framed in reference to those eastern enemies.

In the Assizes of Jerusalem,* traffic in arms is prohibited, under the penalty of death. Similar prohibitions were often issued in Spain, and also in Italy, where they proved of little use. Indeed, Genoa even enriched herself by carrying on an uninterrupted trade in arms with the Levant.

* This work was composed after the Conquest of Jerusalem, in 1099.—TR.

The Germans, at an early period, made much progress in the production of suitable defensive armour. Among the Goths Display of fine armour. in the south of France, the chivalrous display of arms and armour was already remarkable in the fifth century, and remained so throughout the mediæval period. At the wedding procession of the Visigothic Prince Ricimer, the nobles of his suite bore shields inlaid with silver, and adorned with bosses of gold. The splendor and finish of arms at a later period of the middle ages, are sufficiently well known. We merely advert to one specimen kept in Dresden, and made at a time when artistic refinements were but little regarded, and chiefly required for the decoration of churches. The article we allude to is a dagger, (Plate 14, Fig. 3.) made within the latter half of the 11th century. It formed part of the arms of Duke Rodolph of Suabia, when he fought against the Emperor Henry IV. in the battle of Merseburg. The handle of the dagger has, in addition to gilt ornaments, some carving, which, considering the age, reveals great progress in the plastic art, and marks the contrast which continued to exist in the thirteenth and fourteenth centuries, between the elegant instruments of war, and the rude ill-shapen utensils of common life.

The improvements of defensive armour raised the art of protection above the art of destruction. The decoration of arms Arms and Arts. kept even pace with the progress of the formative arts. All extensive armouries contain specimens by Italian masters, which are admired, both for appropriateness of form, and beautifully designed gilt tracings. Drawings on shields, helmets, and horse-coverings, represent battles and other bold achievements, with as much distinctness as is afforded by embossed figures. It is chiefly on shields, that ornaments, consisting of arabesques or armorial bearings, are to be seen (Plates 26, 27).

The most appropriate division of the several pieces of arms is that Division of Armour. suggested by the ancient German designation of offensive and defensive weapons (*Schutz und Trutz Waffen*). The offensive weapons include various missiles, cutting and thrusting instruments, bows, cross-bows, javelins, lances, partisans, mallets, clubs, battle-axes, and so on. The others include helmets, coats of mail, sheathings for the arms and legs, gauntlets, hauberks, shields, and horse-armour.

BOWS, CROSSBOWS, AND ARROWS.

See Plate 1.

The bow, the simplest shooting instrument, was in use among the early Germans, as among all other primitive nations. But, in Bows. all probability, it ceased to be the chief weapon of the Germans, when they overthrew the Roman empire. The battle axe, and the spear are mentioned by Sidonius Apollinaris as the only practical weapons of the Goths. At a later time, the Hungarians gained an ascendancy over the Germans by their skilful use of the bow. The defeat of the Anglo-Saxons, at the battle of Hastings, in some measure, is attributable to the superior skill of the Norman archers. Though the German freemen and feudal nobles do not seem to have applied the bow in their battles, excellency in archery was, nevertheless, considered as a great accomplishment, if we may judge from the statement of a chronicler, who praises Frederic Barbarossa's skill in handling the bow.

About the reign of that monarch, the crossbow (*arcubalista, arbaleste, ballestra*), came into fashion, first among the English and Crossbows. Italians, then among the French and Germans. It remained popular throughout the middle ages. Even in the sixteenth century, it was not altogether abandoned by the disciplined armies, who then were already supplied with fire-arms. Among the Scandinavians and their descendants, who settled in France, the bow was held in high estimation. In cases of hostile invasion, of murder, or of robbery, it was the custom among the Scandinavians, to let an arrow go round, as a symbolical summons to the levy of the army.

In the 12th century, when the crossbow came into general use, bows were not given up altogether. Even in England, where the crossbow formed the principal weapon, the bow was retained. Henry VII., who gave his preference to the plain bow, caused his parliament to prohibit the use of the crossbow, or, at least, to restrict its use to the most opulent landed proprietors. In consequence of this restriction, the simple bow again became the weapon of the common orders, in their practices of archery. The crossbow is of ancient invention, though not wielded, at first, by single individuals. Most likely, it originally was a copy, in a reduced scale, of the projecting engines, which were conveyed on cars in the train of the Roman legions.

Vegetius mentions, among those engines, a Balista for discharging arrows. It consisted, most likely, of a large bow, fitted on a beam, and is termed by that author, arcubalistar (See Plate 3, Fig. 1.) The invaders of the Roman empire became acquainted with these engines, which afterwards were manufactured in the cities of Italy, especially in Genoa, where they were made of a small size, so that a single individual could manage them instead of ordinary bows. The Genoese are considered the first who brought the crossbow into extensive use.

It is uncertain when the crossbow was adopted by the Germans. Crossbows in England. In England, it became known in the time of Richard I., and in France, somewhat later. During the third crusade, Richard I. introduced this weapon amongst his subjects. After his death, the crossbow became popular; though it was deemed contrary to the current notions of honour and fairness, that missiles should be hurled from a distance, without the aid of physical force, personal courage, or the dexterity of single combat. Similar objections were entertained at the introduction of gunpowder. The Roman See, indeed, prohibited the crossbow, and threatened the archers with excommunication, but the interference of the Papal court proved of little avail in matters of this kind. Only in France, where the aristocracy and the system of feudalism had a greater influence than anywhere else, a deeply rooted aversion to the crossbow continued to prevail, until the battles of Crecy, Poitiers, and Agincourt rendered it almost an imperative duty to meet the enemy with his own weapons. The rising popularity of the crossbow is incidentally proved by the clauses inserted in the charters of cities; provisions being made that the citizens should be exercised in the management of this weapon. The French, who, before the battle of Agincourt, had employed the services of Genoese archers, subsequently acquired some skill in the use of the crossbow. In 1425, the Duke of Bretagne issued an ordonnance enjoining the adoption of the crossbow, and in 1448, Charles VII. established a corps of Franc-Archers.

To this effect, every parish was required to furnish the best archers, Franc-Archers. who, in return for their military services, were relieved from all civil and local burdens. Such a corps was still in existence in the reign of Louis XI., but in the days of Charles VIII., it gradually declined, though archers are mentioned as late as 1511. In England, the crossbow proved of considerable value to the army of Edward I. This monarch, in subjecting the Welch, gained a complete victory over Prince Llewellyn, partly by the aid of archers, who, being mounted and distributed among the knights, sallied forth to give battle. At Crecy, the defeat of the French arose from the superiority of the English over the French and Genoese arbalisters.

At Poitiers, crossbow-men took a decisive part in the issue of the battle. At Agincourt, those archers secured the favourable termination of the battle, though this was more owing to stratagem and the thoughtlessness of the French, than to the success of archery. English legislation promoted the general adoption of this weapon by the people. An ordonnance of Edward III., which was addressed to the Lord Mayor of London, directed the citizens to practise archery on holidays; and a parliamentary act passed in the reign of Edward IV. extended the same law to the whole kingdom, under the penalty of a pecuniary fine. Many English traditions prove that the crossbow had become a favourite weapon. They almost invariably describe the yeomen with crossbows. As an instance, may be mentioned the armed appearance of Robin Hood. Under Henry VII. and VIII., the use of the crossbow was restricted to the wealthier classes, whose income was not less than £100. Still, its use was not altogether withdrawn from the people; even so late as the seventeenth century, this weapon formed an essential part of public diversions. In Italy, especially in Genoa, the crossbow stood in high favour. Genoese archers served as mercenaries in foreign armies, particularly in those employed by the French. At Crecy, their number amounted to 15,000, and in the service of Bertrand du Guesclin were no less than 10,000. In Aragon, a statute went so far as to determine, that a nobleman's son, who was not himself a knight or a crossbow-man, was not to be admitted at a knight's table.

Though the crossbow was gradually superseded by the musket, it was still commonly used by the armies during the first half of the sixteenth century. Götz von Berlichingen often mentions it, in his autobiography, as the common weapon of his time. In the small corps which accompanied Cortez at the conquest of Mexico, the numbers of musketeers and crossbow-men were equal. When Cortez entered Mexico for the second time, he led eighty musketeers and eighty crossbow-men.

The construction of the crossbow is shown in Plate 1. The bow *Construction of the Crossbow.* was fastened to a stock. This was grooved for the admission of the arrow. The bowstring being fastened to a projecting nut, was let off by the pressure of the hand on the handle underneath the bow. Behind the bow, a " sight" was fixed for regulating the arrow, and at the end of the stock was an iron rest, on which the archer placed his foot, while bending the bow, in order to gain force in drawing up the string of the weapon that rested on the ground and was being turned upwards. At first, bows were made of wood (*Arc d'Aubour*); according to Meyrick, of hazelwood, and of the branches of the Oriental (Syrian) vine tree, which by Venetian merchants, was imported into Europe. Bows were also made of yew or of horn, and afterwards of steel. The string consisted only of plaited gut, and often merely of a hempen cord. There were frequently two strings to the bow. The archers used to carry a couple, which were not always fastened to the bow. The string was originally drawn by the mere force of the arms, but in the 14th century, pulleys came into use, which were fixed to the top of the stock. These drew the string higher up than could have been effected by the unaided hand. Now and then, shafts were adorned with inlaid ivory, or ornamented with carvings. Two bows of this description are delineated in the second volume of Meyrick's work.* He there gives the following description, which seems to apply to the general character of this weapon, and, to a great extent, serves as an explanation of the representation in Plate 1. "The first consists of a large stock made of some very hard wood, stained *Description of the Crossbow.* and curiously, though rudely inlaid with ivory, three feet, three inches in length, one inch three quarters in the thickest part, and five inches three quarters in the deepest; and of a steel bow of about two feet eight inches from end to end, two inches in the deepest part, and nearly three-quarters of an inch thick, weighing fifteen pounds. The bow is fitted into the stock at a distance of four inches and a half from the end, at which place projects a stirrup, seven and a half inches in length, by five and a quarter inches in the widest span. The length of the groove for the quarrel is one foot four inches, including that of the nut, which is above half an inch wide. The nut is of ivory and about two inches

* Page 127.

in diameter, but that it might not obstruct the sight, the stock is hollowed out accordingly from about four and a half inches about it. At the distance of eleven inches from the butt end is an ivory sight, which, being brought with the head of the quarrel into the same straight line as the object, or a little above it, as elevation may or not be requisite, enables the marksman to shoot with certainty. The spring of the trigger, which is within side the stock, is eight inches long; and the trigger itself, which projects from the under part of the stock, is protected by a bar of iron which serves, not only as a guard and to steady the hand, but also as a handle by which to take off the lock. It is furnished with the moulinet and pulleys, which, after the bow had been bent, may be removed for the discharge. These consist of an iron cylinder in a frame of the same metal, made to turn by two movable handles in opposite directions, and having a cap likewise of iron to put on the butt end of the stock. On each side of this cap is a small pulley, the wheel of which is one inch and a half in diameter, having attached to one of its arms, a strong cord, that passes thence round another equal sized wheel, returns over the first, and then goes round one double in diameter, situated beyond the second described, and so passes to the cylinder of the moulinet, by winding which the power required to bend the bow, is lessened to a fourth. Attached to the arms of the greater wheels is a double claw, made to slide on the plane of the stock, which, catching hold of the bowstring, draws it up to the nut."

A bow of this construction was naturally of superior efficiency. The arrows were originally of greater length, and this *Crossbow Arrows.* missive instrument could be increased in weight, and consequently, in force. The iron point was now made thicker, and the stem shorter. These missiles were termed in Germany, *Bolzen*, in England, *Quarrels and Bolts*, and in France, *Quarreaux* (*quadrelli*) on account of their shape, which at first was square. Barbed hooks were added to inflict severe wounds, and these variations in the shape of the quarrels were very considerable. Anticipating that the adversaries were provided with strong defensive armour, less attention was paid to the point, than to the lateral edge and to the weight of the bolt, by means of which characteristics the missile could penetrate the defensive armour. The points represented in Plate 1, partly resemble those of ordinary lances. The trifoliated bolts (Plate 1, Lines 3 and 4) are remarkable for having, probably, suggested the adoption of the lilies in the royal insignia of France. The same Plate also exhibits a heavy bolt and feathered arrows. It was a common practice to furnish the arrows with feathers, to give them a more steady flight when discharged. In some instances, leather and wooden strips replaced feathers. The latter formed important items in the ammunition of war, especially amongst the English, whose armies contained a considerable number of crossbow-men. Hence the British subjects were required to contribute goose-feathers. Under Henry V., during the war with France, an act of Parliament enjoined the sheriffs to procure goose-feathers, six being required from every goose.

The foregoing description proves that the crossbow was a *Effect of* formidable weapon. Yet the knight, in his armour, was *the Crossbow.* not as much exposed to injury as was his horse. In consequence of such dangers, it was that the French nobles, at the battle of Poitiers, fell into confusion. When the force of the pulley was employed to discharge the quarrel, the hauberk itself proved ineffectual. Otterbourne, quoted by Meyrick in Vol. 2, Page 101, gives the following account of Lord Percy's victory over Douglas of Scotland. "The Lord Percy's archers did withal deliver their deadly weapons so lively, so courageously, so grievously, that they ran through the men-at-arms, bored their helmets, pierced their very swords, beat their lances to the earth, and easily shot those who were more slightly armed through and through."

An oriental historian, quoted by Meyrick, under the heading of Richard I., notices the superiority of the western crossbow-men over the Turkish archers. This superiority accounts for the retention of the crossbow so late as the first half of the 16th century, when the musket could not be handled with the same facility as the pulley-drawn crossbow, which had a range of forty rods.

The equipment of the crossbow-men varied. On the tapestry *Equipment of* of Bayeux, archers, both mounted and on foot, are *Crossbow-men.* represented in complete chain-mail hauberks, which descended to the knees. The covering of the head consisted of a closely fitting helmet without visor. The latter was added afterwards, when the helmet was shaped conically, with a projecting back-piece. At the same time, the armour was made to cover the lower part of the legs and the feet. Troops, furnished with the weapon just mentioned, could only enumerate few crossbow-men in complete armour. Many merely wore a pectoral, *i.e.*, breast-plate, or a ringed hauberk, which covered the body and part of the legs. Others were dressed in leather coats, to which were attached circular metal plates, generally four, for protection or for ornament. Archers are thus represented in the illustrations of a M.S. copy of Froissart's Chronicles; they have four metal plates on the breast and two on the elbows. Persons, thus attired, were followed in battle by special attendants, who protected them with large shields, called pavise or pavois. These were of a man's height, half-curved, and terminated in a point, so as to be stuck into the ground. Some crossbow-men carried their arrows in quivers, and others wore them in the belt. They were mostly provided with a sword of moderate length, and with a mace, or battle-axe. The ordonnance of the Duke of Bretagne, on the establishment of archers, directs that they should supply themselves with a bow, quiver, cappeline, (i.e., skull cap) coustille, (which served the purpose of knife and dagger) axe, or maule of lead, strong jacks, furnished with little plates of iron, chain, or mail, to cover their arms. And those who were unacquainted with the art of shooting, should be armed with jacks, and have cappelines, coustilles, axes, or bouges, (*i.e.*, long bladed swords, affixed to the end of a pole), paniers of aspen, or other wood, the most suitable they could find, and that these paniers should be long, so as to cover them above and below. This shield was used instead of the pavises, which usually consisted of wooden boards strengthened with iron bars. In fortified castles or cities, the crossbow-men wore no armour. They stood behind the battlements or embrasures; hence they were called by the French *crennequiniers*, from *crenequin* (battlement). The crossbows were, in some rare instances, used for the projection of leaden balls, besides arrows. Sometimes, at sieges, fiery arrows were *Missiles* discharged; these missiles were covered with combustible *discharged.* materials, (as for example, with flax, steeped in pitch or rosin), and were set on fire. Combustible fluids in small phials, were sometimes attached below the arrow-heads.* In a symbolical point of view, the arrow, among the Lombards, served as the sign of manumission. The arrow was solemnly handed over to the manumitted slave, most likely to indicate that henceforth he would be entitled to carry arms. This custom remained in force when the bow had ceased to be a popular weapon.

* See Plate 1.

PROJECTING ENGINES, BATTERING RAMS, AND MOVABLE TOWERS.

Plates 3, 4, 5, 6, 7.

The projecting engines, like all other instruments of siege, were of very ancient origin, and derived from the Romans. The _{Towers.} barbarian invaders very soon became proficient in handling the warlike implements of the Roman legions. In the 5th century, already, the Goths and Vandals, attacked the Romans with those ancient destructive machines. Even the Huns, the most savage of the barbarians who overran the empire, were not slow in discovering the advantages of these engines of war. Attila took Aquileia by the help of these machines. The Arabs, also made use of them, probably on coming in contact with the Byzantines. In 711 and 712, at the siege of Merida, and Seville, the last towns in which the Spanish Goths offered some resistance, the Arabs made use of wooden towers and other war engines, in storming and destroying the fortifications. Until the period, when the invention of gunpowder altered the whole method of warfare, these engines were common to all the western nations, and, like the crossbow, they, for some time, continued in use at sieges, after the new artillery had come into vogue. The Turks, on investing Constantinople, combined the ancient with the modern artillery. Cannons worked together with machines which ejected stones and arrows. The bullet and the battering ram helped to destroy the wall. The Turks made also a fruitless attempt to ascend the wall by means of a wooden tower, which was constructed in imitation of siege towers, built by the Romans and the occidental nations. Similar engines occur even at a later age. The Spaniards, under Gonsalvo de Cordova, employed them in Naples; and Cortez, in besieging Mexico, attempted the construction of a machine to bear upon the houses of the enemy. The Turks seem to have used these engines at a much later date. In the 18th century, hurling engines were seen by Baron de Tott in the arsenal of Constantinople. The Italians possessed the greatest skill in the manufacture of these engines. The wooden towers by means of which the Crusaders stormed Jerusalem, were of Genoese workmanship. The makers of the engines were called "*artillatores;*" their art was termed "*artilleria.*"

The projecting engines were invented by the Alexandrian Greeks, and imitated by the Romans, through whom they _{Origin of the} became known to the barbarians. Some of these engines _{Projecting Engines.} shot off arrows or ejected stones and balls; those of the first description are delineated in Plate 3, Fig. 1 & 2. They were termed Arcubalistæ, which, as has already been stated, gave origin to the crossbow. At sieges, the machine rested either on fixed frame-works, (see Fig. 2 of the Plate) or the framework itself rested on wheels to facilitate the transport of the machine. As in the crossbow, a pulley was used for drawing the string (Fig. 2). The latter consisted of cords made of gut. The arrow was often of the size of a beam, and its force depended on the dimensions of the bow. The machines for ejecting stones mainly consisted of a perpendicularly suspended beam. It was held down at one end by means of twisted ropes, and at the opposite side it was balanced by a heavy weight of stones or metal, which caused a violent recoil of the beam, as soon as its basis was detached, or released by cutting the rope. The missiles were usually put into a hollow space, and discharged from the beam as soon as this was made to recoil, by the weight suspended underneath. Plate 4, Fig. 4 represents the machine drawn up; Fig. 5 exhibits it in the act of ejecting the missiles. The construction of this engine displays some skill. The beam is pointed. The counterpoise, consisting of stones, is contained in cases which turn on hinges. Meyrick (Vol. 1, P. 170) has a representation of a more clumsy machine. During the middle ages, these engines were called *Mangana, Petrariæ,* and *Trebucheta,* (*mangonels, perrieres,* and *trabuquets*).

The petraries and mangonels are always distinguished from each other by William of Tyre, in his history of the Crusades. _{Petraries and} His work suggests that the petrary was used for ejecting stones, _{Mangonels.} and the manganum for darting. At a later period, the French writers, employed the word *Mangoneaux* as the general designation of projecting engines. The German name of manganum was *Springard, i. e.,* the jerking or slinging engine.

These engines, being slow in action, and difficult of transport, subsequently gave way to the superior force of fire-arms. _{Force of the} Yet, their effect was by no means to be despised, as we _{Projecting Engines.} may judge from the following facts mentioned by a contemporaneous chronicler. During the third crusade, Richard Cœur de Lion caused a number of such machines to be constructed, which did considerable damage to the Turks. A single stone, slung from such an engine, killed twelve men, and was pointed out to Saladin as a curiosity. Stones thus thrown were capable of breaking walls, and for this reason were combined with other implements of assault. For this purpose, they were often especially shaped. The projectiles, sometimes made of burnt clay, were, most likely, required in battles. In some instances they were of iron. Metal balls were occasionally made hollow, and filled with combustible materials, in order to set fire to the buildings of the besieged cities, or to the wooden towers of the besiegers. By such means, the so-called Greek fire used to be thrown forth.

Greek Fire. The Greek fire seems to have been invented by the Byzantines, in the seventh century, when the power of the Caliphs threatened to overthrow the Oriental Empire. The inventor is said to have been a Syrian Greek, who, in his flight, on the approach of the Arabs, took refuge in Constantinople. By this timely invention, Byzantium was, for centuries, delivered from the ascendancy of the Moslems. Through the agency of this fire, the Arabs were twice compelled to desist from the siege of Constantinople. For four centuries, the Oriental portion of the Roman Empire succeeded in keeping secret the ingredients of this destructive power; but in the eleventh century, the Arabs and Turks became acquainted with its preparation, which, for some time, continued to be a mystery to the occidental nations. During the Crusades, this fire afforded the same advantage to the Turks over their western enemies, as it formerly had afforded to the Greeks over the Arabs. At the siege of Acre, its use was already known to the Turks. It served to ignite the siege towers, was used in sea fights, and was employed also in repelling the assaults of the besiegers.

Its effect on the army of St. Louis in Egypt was terrific. Joinville describes, with great simplicity, the panic of that army which had defied the swords and lances of the Saracens. The French were stupified, as it were, when the Greek fire was hurled at them. According to that writer, it flew through the air in the shape of a huge winged dragon, with the glare of lightning, and the report of thunder, rending the darkness of the night with its flame. There is no subsequent instance on record of the vehement and decisive effect of this fire. It was probably after the invention of gunpowder, that the use of Greek fire was relinquished. A physician, who lived in the reign of Edward III., describes the mode in which this fire was prepared. As regards its nature, ancient writers agree that its flames could only be extinguished by vinegar and urine, mixed with sand. It is also said, that it possessed destructive power, and that its flame did not rise in a straight line, but diffused itself on all sides. It was sent forth by means of hollow balls, arrows, or copper tubes. The latter were, for this purpose, carried in the ships of the Byzantines. The fire was thrown from large pots, if the enemy made an attempt to scale the walls. It was also hurled along in bottles, and other fragile vessels.

The composition of this igniting material varied with its solid or liquid state. The Byzantines, who make mention of the composition, give purposely, as it seems, an inexact description of it. Ingredients of the Greek Fire. According to Anna Comnena, combustible rosins and oils, especially naphtha, were its chief component parts. Anderne, who lived in the time of Edward III., describes its composition as follows: " Take of sulphur vivum, 1 lb., of colophony (common rosin) 1 lb., of pitch, used for naval purposes, 1 quarter, of extract of opoponax, (a gum resin, obtained by wounding the roots of the pastinaca opoponax, a plant of the Levant) 1 quarter, of pigeon's dung well-dried, 1 quarter; let all the before-mentioned be well pulverised, and then resolve them in turpentine water or oil of sulphur vivum (oil of vitriol); and then put them altogether into a glass vessel, the mouth of which should be well closed, and put that vessel for fifteen days in a hot oven: afterwards distil the whole in the manner of spirits of wine, and keep it for use." In another place, the same writer states that the Greek fire chiefly consisted of turpentine water, slowly distilled with turpentine gum, and that it was ignited by throwing water upon it.

Hoyer, in his History of Tactics, (*Geschichte der Kriegskunst*) suggests that the composition of Greek fire must have contained saltpetre, this being the only inflammable substance which possesses explosive properties, and is capable of being discharged in an horizontal direction. If saltpetre was really used in the preparation of Greek fire, the composition of gunpowder may have resulted from experiments with that explosive substance.

The engines used at sieges consisted of towers, battering rams, and movable sheds (*Vineæ*) for the protection of archers and miners. **Movable Towers, Battering Rams, and Sheds.** The western nations, on invading the Roman empire, imitated the engines of the Romans, who either adopted them from the Greeks, or after their war with Pyrrhus, improved upon the former attempts of the successors of Alexander.

The ancient machines differed but little, if at all, from those of the middle ages; the figures represented in Plates 5, 6, and 7, have, therefore, been copied from the designs of Folard, who has sketched them from the descriptions of the ancients. Plate 5 represents the movable tower of Cæsar, in the siege of Namur. It moved upon rollers. **Cæsar's Tower.** Every windlass required twelve men to put the machine into motion. Plate 6 exhibits a tower with galleries, and a battering ram. Plate 7 represents the tower of Demetrius Poliorcetes, at the siege of Rhodes, which was fitted with drawbridges. Figure 1 of that plate shows the ground-plan of the tower. Figure 2 is a view of a caster or roller, and its appurtenances; *d* is the roller, supported in a framework *c*, to which the rod *b* is connected; *g* is a stay; *f* marks the supports of the tower.

Vegetius describes this species of war engine in the following manner: "The tower consists of beams and planks, which are covered with hides to protect them from catching fire. It is from thirty to fifty feet in width, and higher than the invested fortifications. It moves on rollers. The lower part contains the battering ram, the drawbridge is in the middle, the top is occupied by slingers and archers." The mediæval towers differed from the Roman merely in being furnished with parapets and battlements, behind which the archers were stationed. Meyrick gives the following description of such a tower, from a design of a manuscript in the British Museum. "It is composed of a huge frame of timber, placed on small rollers; open from the first floor downwards, probably for the convenience of moving with greater facility. The top is embattled with embrasures, each furnished with a lid or shutter; two upright timbers issue out of the centre of the tower, by means of which a large bridge is suspended in the air, with the foremost edge inclined like a roof, to serve the purpose of an immense pavis, or mantlet, and protect the soldiers stationed on the battlements, from the arrows of the besieged. These uprights were constructed so as to be capable of dropping jointly forward, in the two foremost embrasures of the tower, while, by some mechanical power, the bridge was, at the same time, poised in a horizontal direction, and projected upon the ramparts of the besieged." The construction of the bridge differs somewhat from that depicted in Plate 7. The bridge is fixed to the top, and is supported below by beams. Such towers, termed in mediæval Latin, *Belfredus, Belfragium, Bastia, Bastida,* and in French, *Beffroy Bastide, &c.,* were used in many sieges throughout the middle ages. The Crusaders employed such towers in the conquest of Jerusalem. The English built engines of this kind three stories high; each story could hold one hundred arbalisters, in addition to the heavy-armed men. The whole building appears to have afforded space for five hundred men. These towers were sometimes removed to great distances. William the Conqueror, for example, is said to have brought some to England.[*] Sometimes, the besieged, at the approach of the towers, raised the wall to a greater height. The upper stories of the towers were, therefore, so arranged, as to be drawn higher up, as soon as the movable fabric had arrived at its place of destination. Before moving the towers to the ramparts of fortified places, it was necessary to fill up the ditches.

This labour was performed under the shelter of sheds, such as, by the Romans, were termed *Vineæ*, and which commonly bore the name of "cats." **"Cats."** They consisted of boards and hides. The sides were supported by the insertion of cane. From a description Vegetius has given of the *Vinea*, it is evident that the Germans learnt the use of this contrivance from the Romans. That author mentions engines of this kind by the name of "*catti.*" The Germans denominated them "*Katzen,*" the French, "*chats,*" and the Spaniards, "*gatos.*" Du Cange supposes that this shed received such a name in consequence of the soldiers lying under it in wait like cats. Such a protecting engine was pushed forward, when mines were to be dug for the purpose of making a breach in the ramparts. Wooden pillars, covered with pitch, tar, and other combustibles, helped to support the mines. As soon as the subterranean passage was completed, the pillars were set on fire.

---

[*] Verstegan informs us that William the Conqueror, on his first arrival in England, set up "three castles of wood, which had been made and framed in Normandy."—Meyrick, I., 14.

The battering ram (*aries*) consisted of one or more beams, joined Battering Rams. together and armed at one end with iron, formed in the shape of a ram's head. It was suspended by the middle, and hanging equally balanced, it was drawn back and then again thrust forward against the wall. This machine, which was much used by the Romans, was called in mediæval Latin, *Berbix*, a corrupt derivation from *Vervex*. Its French name was *Berbice*. It was mostly placed in the lower story of the movable tower, or sheltered beneath a shed. Its apex was bent for the purpose of penetrating easily into the joints of the wall and pulling out the stones. To lessen the effect of these machines, towers were built in a circular form. The besieged frequently endeavoured to arrest the force of the battering rams by means of hooks attached to levers.

The principal resistance to the attacks of movable towers and to Greek Fire. the working under sheds, consisted in the attempt of setting fire to the engines. The exertions of the Crusaders before Acre were frequently frustrated by the Greek fire, with which the Saracens burned down many works of their adversaries. This engine was employed by the Turks at the siege of Constantinople. Sultan Mahmoud, after having severely injured the wall near the gate of St. Romanus, ordered that a tower, far exceeding the height of the wall, should be moved onward. The moat was already filled up; before, however, the tower could be pushed against the wall, night had set in. The Turks had the intention of continuing the attack on the following day. But the Greeks availed themselves of the darkness of the night to burn the siege engine, to restore the damaged wall, and to empty the ditch. Attempts to extinguish the fire, by covering the tower with wet hides, were fruitless, and the Turks were obliged to desist from this operation. Scaling ladders were used now and then. In these cases, the knights, protecting themselves with their shields, took the lead in ascending the ladders. During the siege of Jerusalem, such means were employed by the Crusaders to take the city, but proved unsuccessful.

SPEARS, LANCES, HALBERTS, AND PARTIZANS.

Plates 8, 9, 10, 11.

The spear being the simplest weapon of attack, was known to most of the barbarous nations. Tacitus mentions it under the Spears and Lances. name of *framea*, as the principal weapon of the Germans. The name of lance occurs in ancient German dialects, and like the majority of armorial terms, it has been introduced into the Romanesque languages. Roman authors, whose writings treat of the subversion of their country, allude to the spear, as one of the principal weapons of the Germans. It appears that the spear was then, no longer hurled from a distance, but merely thrust in closer conflict. The javelin, which was much lighter, belongs to a later period. It very likely originated in the East, and was, through the medium of the Spaniards, communicated to the western nations. Among the feudal nobles, the lance was considered as one of the most dignified weapons, and its use was denied to plebeians. William the Conqueror granted to his feudal nobles, the privilege of using the lance. In France, during the time of St. Louis, commoners were only, on some special occasions, permitted to carry the spear of the heavy-armed warriors, which was then generally designated as a lance. Weapons of this kind were then exceedingly long and heavy. The shafts were made of the wood of the aspen, lime, pine, sycamore, or ash trees. The gripes of lances were occasionally hollow, and covered with expensive woven material. Meyrick describes a lance, which was covered with crimson velvet. The iron blade generally was blunt, rather ponderous, and broad. That writer also mentions a lance-head, made in the time of William the Conqueror, which is 8 inches broad, and from 12 to 14 inches long.

Below the head of the lance, a flag, the Gonfanon, was fixed, which indicated the rank of the bearer, and also contributed to terrify the horses of the adversaries. In the Bayeux Gonfanon. tapestry, William the Conqueror is represented with a small red and blue flag, which terminates in three indentations. At a later time, the Bannerets (*Chevaliers Bannerets*) carried a square banner under their lances. A small round conical shield of iron, termed *vamplate*, was screwed above the gripe of the lance, for the protection of the hand. During the tournament the lance-head was removed and replaced by the so-called crown, which consisted of three short and blunt iron staves. These were placed in divergent directions, and projected from a small iron-plate.

The Chronicles of the ages of chivalry compute the strength of an army by the number of knights' lances. The Romance of Parthenopex, moreover, informs us, that lances, fixed in the ground, before the camp-tents of knights, indicated the rank of their owners.

The spear had a symbolical signification. Being contrasted with Spears as the spindle and distaff, it represented the male sex. Kings Symbols. gave a spear to their heirs, as a sign of the transfer of power. According to Gregory of Tours, King Gunthram, handed one to his son, Childebert, telling him that thereby, he conferred upon him the dominion of the whole empire. Spears were, in some instances, regarded as equal to the sceptre. During the war with Rodolphe of Suabia, the Emperor Henry IV. granted to the Duke of Bohemia the royal dignity by means of a lance, which, at a subsequent period in the middle ages, was carried at public ceremonials, before the Dukes of Bohemia. The chieftains in the Highlands of Scotland, made use of the spear termed *cranntair*, to spread alarm and gather the vassals around them. The cranntair is explained by Armstrong as being a piece of half-burnt wood, dipped in blood. Customs, somewhat similar, were observed by the Romans and also by the Scandinavians. The spear, with a key attached to it, when sent to the enemy, was the sign of the surrender of those who were besieged in a city or a castle. Such a surrender is represented in the Bayeux tapestry. Spears forming an essential part in the equipment of knights, descended as inestimable heirlooms to the posterity of renowned warriors. We may mention, as a valued relic of this description, the spear of Charlemagne, with which he had fought against the Saracens. It formed part of some precious gifts presented by Hugh of France to King Athelstane.

Besides the knightly spear, there were also pointed weapons of various Varieties kinds. Some are depicted in Plates 8, 9, 10, and 11. The of Spears. Fig. 5 and 6 of the eighth Plate appear to represent hunting spears. It is improbable that before the introduction of feudalism, a great difference should have existed between the war-spear and the hunting-spear. It was only when the heavy-armed cavalry of the feudal nobility required a weapon for vigorous thrusts, that a new and suitable shape was devised. The foot soldier could not conveniently have wielded this ponderous piece of arms, even had it not been appropriated by the horsemen. So soon, however, as the importance of foot soldiers began to be felt, these warriors received spears of a new kind, consisting of long slender staves, with longer and thinner heads, and this class is known under the name of lances. The arms, represented in Plates 9, 10, and 11, chiefly belong to a later time. Until the 15th century, spears were of a more simple shape. At first, especially in the 12th century, an iron hook was added to the lance (the *oncin*), in order to pass easily through the rings of the armour. In the 12th century, lances were made without pointed heads, and the infantry was armed with hooks affixed to long staves. The menial orders, when serving in war, carried such implements. At an early period, the lance of the foot soldiers was so constructed as to represent a double weapon. In the twelfth century, it had two or three heads, which were either fixed to the extremity of the shaft, or were thrown out by the pressure of a spring. Meyrick states, that some weapons of this kind had spikes of three feet in length. (See Plates 10 and 11). An axe was sometimes attached to the lance. This was the case before foot soldiers were supplied with partizans and halberts. Such weapons, known under the appellation of *Bisarme, Gisarme,* or *Jusarme,* consisted of lance-heads, and had curved blades for the purpose of cutting. In England, and probably in all other parts of the west, this species Gisarme. of weapon was peculiar to infantry. In the Winchester statutes, this weapon is appropriated to the inferior orders of the people, whose land is below the value of 40 shillings.

When the infantry had regained its former importance by the accession of the citizens of Germany, Italy, and Switzerland, the spear became a favourite weapon, and the chivalric lance lost its popularity. This was especially the case, when the regular and closed columns of Swiss infantry, with their pikes, (long and slender lances) repelled the impetuous assaults of the harnessed cavalry. The Italian mercenaries, who fought as foot soldiers under their leaders, the so-called *Condottieri*, were equally victorious in defeating with spontoons or broad-bladed spears, the heavy-armed horsemen, who were collected from the chivalrous adventurers of all nations.

The chivalric lance gradually disappeared. Even the commanding officers of infantry gave their preference to the pikes, which had been modified from the gisarme, and in the fourteenth century, were introduced in Germany under the names of partizans or halberts. The etymology of the word partizan suggests that this weapon was of French or Italian invention, since *partisane*, or *pertuisane*, seems connected with the verb *pertuiser* or *pertugiare*, to pierce. German and Swiss mercenaries introduced the partizan in the French army during the reign of Louis XI. In England, this weapon only became popular under Henry VIII., and it gave way to the bayonet, which was invented in the reign of Louis XIV. The use of this weapon was discontinued by the majority of the English army during the reign of William III.

Partizans and Halberts.

Specimens of partizans are given in Plate · 8, Fig. 3 & 4. The staff was five or six feet long, and the lower end was mounted with iron. The head consisted of a broad double-edged blade, to which was attached a crescent-shaped instrument for cutting, and a sharp hook on the opposite side. The halbert and the partizan were constructed on the same principle. It is possible that the former merely differed from the other in being lighter, thinner, more pointed, and in having a cutting bill.

Javelins were not much used by the nations of German extraction, though occasional notice of them occurs in Tacitus, and among the Frisians in the thirteenth century. Those who often came in contact with the Orientals, as, for example, the Venetians and the Spaniards, appear to have employed them. The Venetians, by a skilful management of this weapon, gained a naval victory over the Neapolitan Normans. The Spaniards were, throughout the middle ages, so famed for throwing the javelin, that the French, in the fifteenth century, called this weapon *Javelin d'Espagne*, or *Janetaire*, from the Spanish *Gineta*. The javelin was also known to the nations of Celtic origin. The Welch, with this weapon, successfully opposed the English until the reign of Edward I. The Irish troops in the service of the English, were armed with this weapon until a still later period.

Javelins.

SWORDS AND DAGGERS.

Plates 12, 13, 14, 15, 16.

Both in practice and in a symbolical sense, the sword formed the most important part of chivalric armament. It received that shape already from the ancient Germans, which it retained throughout the middle ages. The greater number of the nations who invaded the western empire termed this weapon *Spada* or *Spatha*, a name which, with various modifications, was retained in all the Romanesque languages. Among the Cimbri, it is said to have been broad, long, and pointless, thus differing from the short Roman and Spanish swords. During the decline of the empire, the use of the small sword was discontinued. Vegetius calls this sword by its German name. According to Isidorus, it was known to the Goths, under the name of *Scrama*. Ordericus Vitalis notices it among the Vandals. The Saxons owed their national name to the dagger-shaped sax (*seax*). Meyrick enumerates various descriptions of this weapon. He mentions the shining sword, the sharp-pointed sword, the dull or pointless sword, the two-edged, and the broad sword.

Swords.

The Germans retained the ancient shape of the sword for a much longer period than the other nations. French writers, such as Joinville, speak of the sword, in its primitive shape, as the " German sword." In the fourteenth century, this species of arms was imported into France from Lubeck, and known under the name of " *Glaive de Lubeck.*" Its ancient form is exhibited in the Plates 12, Fig. 3 & 4, and 13, Fig. 3. Generally it had but one edge with a broad back, and was wielded with both hands. The grasp was half the length of the hilt, between the cross and the pommel; the rest being merely a bar of iron, which terminated by a large circular pommel to counterpoise the weight of the blade. The top of the blade was either semi-circular, or of an obtuse angle. Double-edged blades came into use in the fourteenth and fifteenth centuries. They considerably exceeded in length those of the present time. Meyrick mentions a sword of the length of ten palms. Plate 13, Fig. 2 & 3, exhibits two swords. The first belonged to Henry the Pious, Duke of Silesia, and is six feet long; the other was the property of John George I., Elector of Saxony, and measures five feet in length.

Besides the German sword, the French used the *épée à l'estoc*, or stabbing sword, which terminated in a point. In German, this kind of arms was called "*Panzerstecher.*" The Franks of the earliest period seem to have had a very short but broad sword. One of this class, depicted in Plate 16, Fig. 5, is deposited in St. Denis. Doubtful tradition attributes it to Charlemagne. Montfaucon has given delineations of a similar sword, which correspond with one found during the last century in the tomb of the Frankish king, Childeric. In the 15th century, swords were made with flaming blades. Meyrick is of opinion that they were mainly for show on state occasions, but he admits, that in some instances, they were used in battle, especially by the Switzers. (See Plate 12, Fig. 1 & 2).

Falchion. The falchion (*falcastrum*, in French, *fauchon*) is exhibited in Plate 15, Fig. 4. It had a curved blade, and was more common than the other shapes of the sword. The Crusaders, on coming in contact with the Saracens, probably made it popular among the Occidentals. In Spain, this curved weapon was in high favour. During the later part of the middle ages it was very generally worn, as is proved by many passages in Du Cange's glossary, though it does not seem to have been used by knightly warriors in Europe. During the crusades, however, they do not appear to have disdained the use of the falchion. Robert of Normandy fought with one at the siege of Antioch. The sword here depicted, belonged to Thomas Münzer,* and is deposited in Dresden. Another sword of the same kind is shown in Plate 16, Fig. 2. It was carried by the Bohemians in the wars of the Hussites, and was called Dusack, Duseg, or Duseggen. Meyrick mentions a large two-handed sword, with curved blade. Such weapons, however, were of rare occurrence. Swords of smaller dimensions are known under various designations, as for example, the *Vaselars* of the arbalisters, and the above-mentioned *épée à l'estoc*. An additional sword, probably of a smaller size, was attached to the pommel of the knight's saddle, though it is uncertain whether the precaution of carrying an extra sword was commonly adopted. A description of the art of war, copied by Meyrick, from the 4th volume of the Antiquarian Repository, directs that a knight should have two swords, one in his belt, and one on his saddle bow. Joinville, giving an

* Münzer, a notorious fanatic, was the leader of the formidable peasant riots in Thuringia. He was executed in 1525.—TR.

account of the disastrous battle in which his king was made a prisoner, says of himself, that in an encounter with a Saracen, he was pressed against the neck of his horse, which prevented him from drawing the sword; he, therefore, was compelled to use the weapon attached to the pommel. We have also the testimony of Götz von Berlichingen, that he himself was armed both with a long and a short sword.

At the commencement of the 16th century, the sword was reduced in size, and received the form of the modern one-handed weapon. One-handed Sword. Meyrick is of opinion that the change in the size of the sword took place in the reign of the Emperor Maximilian I., when the whole system of arms underwent a revolution.

The light sword (*Degen*) doubtlessly originated in Italy, and became more generally known through the Spaniards, who carried on an extensive trade in the blades which were termed *Toledanos*, owing to the manufactories of arms established in Toledo. The design in Plate 15, Fig. 3, is copied from a sword carried by Dr. Martin Luther, perhaps while he was concealed in the Wartburg, under the assumed name of Junker Görge. This sword is now preserved in Dresden. When the former defensive arms were discontinued, and a new method of fencing came into practice, the hilt was furnished with one or more guards, or with a small circular shield. The two-handed sword, owing to its weight and construction, was better adapted to single combat than any other weapon. Guiart, in his rhymed chronicle, describes the terrible blows the Germans, at the battle of Bovines, inflicted on the French by means of these swords. He relates of Charlemagne, that with his sword, he could cleave a knight right down to the pommel of the saddle, and cut into the very back of the charger. Such statements may be of a fictitious character, yet the efficiency of the weapon is proved by trustworthy contemporaneous authorities. The chroniclers of the first crusade inform us that Godfrey of Bouillon, at the siege of Antioch, cut a Turk into halves from the shoulder down to the hips. A similar feat is attributed by William of Tyre to the Emperor Conrad III. These statements bear evidence that it was not an impossible achievement to cleave or crush the armour of the adversary with a cut of the sword. Du Cange says, that after examining various ancient swords, hung up in churches and convents, he did not discredit the valiant deeds ascribed to Godfrey of Bouillon.

If a knight could wield his ponderous sword with one hand, and keep the other hand disengaged for combat, his skill was much admired. A contemporary of Robert Guiscard relates of that Norman chief, that he went to battle with the sword in one hand and a lance in the other. The sword was usually worn in a belt on the left side. In the Bayeux tapestry, the Normans wear it on the right side. No belt is there to be seen. The closed armour has two apertures, one below the other, to contain the scabbard. The Anglo-Saxons sometimes attached the sword to a scarf descending from the right shoulder. A similar custom was subsequently in fashion among the English and other occidental warriors. Scabbards were, for the most part, made of leather, and occasionally of iron, but in remoter ages, they were often dispensed with. Great care was, at all times, bestowed upon the embellishment of the sword. The girdle *Embellishments and Inscriptions.* and the hilt were often enriched with jewels, or ornamented with gold and silver. Eginhard relates, that Charlemagne in conformity with the fashion of his people, paid great attention to the magnificence of his sword and girdle. The latter as well as the hilt, were covered with precious metals. When the emperor appeared in state, he was armed with a sword, the hilt of which was set with jewels. Some hilts were decorated with embossed work. The swords of the rich were mostly embellished with velvet, fine leather, silver, &c. An inventory of the armory of Louis the Great, King of France, enumerates several swords ornamented with gold, silver, enamel, and velvet. Meyrick has described swords, the knobs of which are enriched with jewels and with bosses of foliage. Swords exhibiting such ornaments are to be seen in Plates 12, Fig. 3, and 13, Fig. 1. The blades frequently contained inscriptions either gilt or simply engraved. Examples of such swords are given in Plates 12, Fig. 1, and 15, Fig. 2. The original of the former is preserved in the armory of Dresden, and is known under the name of "*Kurschwert*" (electoral sword). The hilt is of silver with variously embossed ornaments and partly gilded. Both sides of the blade contain a gilt inscription in relief. One side reads thus: "*Mein Leben und Endt, ist Alles in Gottes Hendt*," A.D. MDCLXVII., *i.e.*, "My life and end are entirely in God's hands." On the other side are the following words: "*Wer mit dem Schwerte ficht, so' werden mit dem Schwert Gericht*," *i.e.*, "He who fights with the sword, shall be judged by the sword." The second

sword has, on one side, the following reading: "*Vor Winter's tet er hochgemuth; Lagarz da haime us er ruht,*" *i.e.*, "Before the winter, he acted spiritedly; this remaining at home he is at rest." On the opposite side, "*Chunrad vil werder Schenke, Hiebie du mir Gedenke,*" *i.e.*, "Conrad, dearest cup-bearer, by this remember me."* The custom of inscribing the blade is still prevalent in Spain. Nearly all Spanish swords, known by the name of "Toledanos," have the following appropriate inscription: "*No me sacas sin razon: no me envainas sin onor,*" *i.e.*, "Do not draw me without a cause: do not ensheath me without honour."

The symbolical importance of the sword manifested itself in various forms and usages which are now partly forgotten. The *Symbolical Usages.* following customs which have been rescued from oblivion, are striking proofs of the high estimation in which this favorite weapon was held by those who were engaged in the performance of significant and solemn acts.

1. Oaths were taken upon the sword. The point was stuck into the ground, and the hand rested on the hilt. The latter was *Oaths.* cruciform, and therefore of a sacred character. After the introduction of Christianity, this custom became widely diffused. Among the Pagan Germans, the blade seems to have been considered as sacred. According to Ammianus Marcellinus, the Quadi took their oaths upon drawn swords. The Pagan Saxons also confirmed their alliances with their naked swords. Some traces of these usages were to be found at a later time in the middle ages, when certain oaths were taken upon the sword instead of the cross. The free-jurors (*Freischöffen*) in the secret tribunals of Westphalia took their oaths while resting their hands on the broad sword. In Holstein, this mode of swearing was retained longer than in any other country.

---

* The recently published *Bildersaal altdeutscher Dichter, &c.*, by Von der Hagen, gives the following correct reading of this inscription, which, on being read, requires three successive turnings.

"CHUNRAT . VIL . WERDER . SHENKE
HIE . BI . DU . MIN . GEDENKE."

On the other side :—

"VON . WINTERSTETEN . HOHGEMUT
LA . GANZ . DEHAINE . IISENHUT."

This means: "Conrad, dearest cup-bearer, hereby remember me." "O valorous Von Wintersteten, leave no iron hat unbroken."—TR.

2. The sword, being solely carried by freemen, became the token of manumission if transferred to dependants or slaves. This mode **Freedom.** of granting freedom was common among the Anglo-Saxons. The sword continued to be worn in England by the members of Parliament at their sittings, and by the jurymen at the assizes, as the sign of political and of judicial authority. This early custom remained in force till late in the seventeenth century.

3. Vanquished warriors, giving themselves up to their antagonists, either came without their swords or held them by their points **Surrender.** and presented the hilts. This mode of surrender implied that the prisoner's life was at the mercy of the victor, as is explained in the ancient French romance, entitled *Le Roman d'Alexandre.*

4. Among the Goths, sons were adopted by means of a sword, which, most likely, was handed over to the adopted individual. **Adoption.** In this manner, Theodoric adopted the king of the Heruli as his son.

5. Among many nations of Western Europe, the sword was the symbol of dominion; for example, among the English, in **Dominion.** the first stages of their monarchy. The kings who preceded Henry III. are represented on their great seals with the sword in their right hands, instead of the sceptre. In Germany, under Frederic I., lands and dominions were symbolically transferred by means of the sword.

6. This weapon was the emblem of justice, especially penal justice. The ancient counts of Germany never attended at court **Justice.** without their swords. The Free Counts were invested with their authority over life and death by receiving a sword and a rope. In Spain, the *Hidalgos de Espada y Horca,* (the nobles of the sword and the gibbet) retained their authority until a very recent date, and superintended the penal jurisdiction in their estates. Of the same class were the swords of state which formed part of the insignia of the crown, and which were, on solemn occasions, carried before the ruling princes. The English had a blunt sword of state in addition to one with a sharp edge. The former, an emblem of mercy, was called *Curteyn,* and belonged to Edward the Confessor.

7. At the nuptials of the Frisians, the sword was employed symbolically. When the bride was about to be conducted **Marriage.** to the bridegroom, a young man, leading the procession, carried in his hand, a drawn sword, which, probably was emblematical, of the authority possessed by the husband over the life of his wife, for he had the option either of striking or of beheading her, if she stood accused of adultery, without being able to clear herself of the suspicion.

8. Among the Franks, the delivery and acceptance of a sword, served as the preliminaries of an impending execution. If the **Sentence of Death.** daughter of a freeman had yielded to the overtures of a slave or a villein, the king or count caused her to chose between a sword and a distaff. If she selected the former, she was obliged to kill the vassal; if she preferred the latter, she was degraded and fell into servitude. According to Gregory of Tours, the kings Childebert and Lothaire, sent a sword and a pair of scissors to the Queen, to choose whether her sons should suffer death, or be deprived of their hair, and enter the convent.

9. In the fifteenth century, a sword sent to an adversary served as a notice of challenge. **Challenge.**

10. A drawn sword was used at marriages by proxy. It was placed in the thalamus between the bride and the representative **Marriage by Proxy.** of the bridegroom. This ancient custom was observed as late as the fifteenth century, when the Duke and subsequent Emperor Maximilian was married by proxy to Mary of Burgundy.

The swords of celebrated combatants, like their lances, were highly valued by succeeding generations, and often bore distinguishing **Swords of Heroes.** proper names. As examples, may be mentioned the sword *Curteyn,* to which we have already referred, and Charlemagne's sword *Joyeuse.* The latter is preserved in the church of St. Denis, and was carried in front of the processions at the coronation of the kings of France. Nearly all heroic legends of that age make mention of swords which bore especial appellations. The Cid, for example, had his *Tizona.* The swords of heroes were carried at their funerals, and then deposited in churches. The sword of Godfrey of Bouillon is kept at his burial-chapel, in the Church of the Holy Sepulchre, where it remains as the only local relic of the crusades. Like Hugh Capet, who thought to honour King Athelstane, by presenting him with the lance of Charlemagne, Richard I. of England offered to Tancred of Sicily, as a precious gift, the pretended sword of King Arthur, which in popular tradition, is known by the name of *Caleburne.*

Sometimes the swords of departed heroes were used in battle. Thus, the Cid girded himself with the sword of the Bastard Mudarra, to avenge an offence done to his father. The Maid of Orleans used a battle-sword which she fetched from the burial vaults of an ancient church.

The dagger was likewise one of the weapons used by the ancient Germans. Its name in the English and in the Romanesque

The Dagger. languages is connected with the German word *Degen*, (sword), which recurs in the French, *Dague*, and in the Spanish, *Daga*. This agreement suggests that this weapon was derived from the Germans. Indeed, it is known, that the Saxons were armed with a short dagger-shaped weapon (the *Sahs*, or in Anglo-Saxon, *Seax* or *Sax*). This name, identical with the national name of the Saxons, was, according to Du Cange, current in the days of Frederic II.* At first, the blade of the dagger seems to have been of greater length and breadth. An old glossary, quoted by Du Cange, explains the word *saxo*, by *semispathium*, i.e., half a sword. In the course of time, the blade of the dagger was made treble-edged and pointed. The French called that weapon *Coustille*, and also *Miséricorde*. Its mediæval Latin name was simply *Cultellum*. This weapon was used in single combat, when knights had vanquished their antagonists, or thrown them to the ground. It was named *miséricorde*, because the unsuccessful enemy was obliged to sue for mercy, if he wished to escape from impending death. It is not improbable that the word miséricorde was applied to the final blow, (the *coup de grace*) in German, *der Gnadenstoss*, by which the defeated adversary was put to death. The dagger formed part of a knight's equipment, and was but rarely omitted. It was worn on the right side, being attached to the hip-belt by a strap or chain. The Normans, as we have observed,

* The researches of this erudite Frenchman need scarcely be consulted on this subject. The mediæval poets of Germany introduce a variety of notices relative to the *Sahs*. In the poem entitled *Annolied*, for example, we meet with the following passage :

　　　　" *ein Duringin duo der siddi was*
　　　　daz si mihhili mezzir hiezin Sahs,"

i.e., " In Thuringia it was usual to call large knives *Sahs*." The word *Sahs*, with its diminutive *Sihhila* (in modern German *Sichel*, in English *Sickle*, in vulgar Latin *Secula*), is considered to be connected with the Latin *secare*, to cut. Grimm ingeniously suggests that the primitive Romans derived from the same word the term *Saxum*, (stone) on account of its being fashioned into cutting instruments. (See his History of the German Language, Vol. II., page 610).—Tr.

wore the sword on the right side, the dagger was therefore fastened on the left. Plate 14, Fig. 3, represents a superior weapon of this class, which belonged to Rodolph, Duke of Suabia. The curved dagger (Plate 16, Fig. 3) was peculiar to the Bohemians. The descendants of the ancient Saxons assigned to the dagger a symbolical meaning. Until a recent period, the Westphalian peasants, when attending their judicial meetings, used to bring knives with them, which they fixed in the ground as a sign of having conformed to the demands of justice. We may here also mention an Italian custom, according to which, the dagger was the symbol of transferring landed property. This custom was probably derived from the ancient Lombards.

BATTLE-HAMMERS, BATTLE-AXES, MARTELS DE FER, MACES, AND SPIKED CLUBS.

Plates 2, 8, 13, 14, 16.

Battle-hammers and battle-axes were the chief weapons of the ancient nations. In ages beyond the reach of written

Battle-har history, stones were used in the construction of these implements of war. Specimens of this kind have been discovere. tombs, as well as in other excavated places, and are now to be seer almost every museum of antiquities. These ancient weapons are represented in Plate 2. Many specimens consist of flint, which, by grinding, takes a keen edge. Barbarous nations in different parts of the world, as for example the *Aztecs*, used this material for similar warlike purposes. Spanish writers state that the edges were not inferior to those of iron in regard to sharpness. The Mexicans could even cut their hair with these stone implements. Grimm has shown that the word hammer (in German, *Streithammer*, i.e., battle-hammer,) originally signified "stone." Northern works of antiquity make it obvious, that the hammer continued to be made of stone, when other arms were already constructed of iron. Battle-hammers were used for the purpose of striking as well as of thrusting. According to the northern mythology, Thor hurls his hammer upon his enemies. This instrument is his chief attribute; on being hurled along, it ever flies back again into his hand.

Under the designation of Martel, this weapon was well known to the Franks, as is evident from the name of Charles Martel, he Martel. having received this name, either for the dexterous use he made of this weapon, or for possessing uncommon strength and prowess. The heavy battle-hammer was in use as late as the fourteenth century. It is said of Bertrand du Guesclin that he used this weapon with both his hands, and made great havoc with it. Amongst the English, the size of the martel was much smaller. One of its sides was blunt, the other sharp. (Plate 13, Fig. 5). Being considered a knightly weapon, it was slung on the saddle or attached to the belt. In England, under Henry VIII., it was carried by officers in command of infantry.

Among the Scandinavians and probably among all Pagan Germans, the hammer, as the attribute of Thor, was a sacred implement. It was used at betrothals, at the consecration of drinking cups, and at funerals. Among some of the Saxon tribes, the hammer was sent round when armed men were summoned to follow the banner of their lord. In Upper Saxony, the custom of circulating the hammer was continued down to modern times, when the people were to be summoned to the hall of justice. In the fourteenth century, a throw of the hammer established the legal title to the boundaries of lands, rivers, and other property. In the Rhine, for example, the jurisdiction of the archbishop of Mayence extended to that distance to which he could fling his hammer while riding into the river.

At the time of the general migration, the Germans used the battle-axe, as a common implement of war. Sidonius Apollinaris relates that the Visigoths had great skill in flinging this weapon, which answered the double purpose of a striking implement and a missile. Among the Franks, the battle-axe bore the name of "*Francisca*," (the Frankish weapon). The same name was given to it by some other German tribes, such as the Goths in Spain, who, most likely, regarded it as of Frankish origin.

The Anglo-Saxons used the battle-axe, as the principal weapon, and seem to have adopted it from the Danes. The latter, as well as the Normans, used a double-edged battle-axe, which was more formidable than the single-edged *Francisca*. Later in the middle ages, the French called the double-edged axes Danish axes (*Haches Danoises*). The handle of such instruments was longer than in those attributed to the Franks. The Lombards appear to have carried a similar long-handled axe, if we may judge by the national name of the tribe, *Longo-bardi*, *i.e.*, bearers of pole-axes. In old German, *Barta* means axe or bill. It occurs in the German word *Hellebarde*, (halbert). The axe is also termed *Hacke*, which is the same as the French *Hache*, and the English *Hatchet*.

Battle-axes with short handles and single blades, as well as with long handles and double blades were in use throughout the middle ages. The battle-axe was a knightly weapon, and some nations held it in the same estimation as the sword. Among the English, in the days of the Tudors, it belonged to the royal insignia, which, on state occasions, were carried before the king. At funerals, it was, together with the helmet and the shield, laid on the altar. Even kings carried it in battle. In Meyrick's work, Richard I. is represented with a battle-axe, as his favourite weapon. King John of France had felled many enemies with that weapon before he was taken prisoner at Poitiers. The axes of Norman commanders were adorned with gold and precious stones, and served as insignia of office. Men of inferior rank were not permitted to carry the battle-axe, the knightly lance, and the broad sword.

The *martel de fer*, which, at a later period, was called by the Germans *Mordhacke* (*i.e.*, homicidal hatchet) was single-bladed, Mordhacke, and furnished with one or more spikes on the opposite side. or Hatchet. The handle was made of iron, or heavily mounted with that metal to increase the force of the blow. Specimens are delineated in Plates 13, Fig. 4, and 14, Fig. 1. The latter figure is the copy of an axe, the edge of which is unusually small. This elegant relic is preserved in Dresden, and was originally the weapon of the Elector John George. The embossed iron hilt exhibits the idolatry of the Jews. The axe itself contains etchings of warlike trophies. Some hilts were furnished with chains to insure a firmer grasp. The same description of battle-axes is to be noticed in that effigy of Richard I, to which reference has been made above.

The club is one of the primitive weapons of the ancient Germans,
The Club.   The morning star or spiked club, though possibly of great
antiquity, does not appear to have been in use before the
eleventh century. The club, originally of wood and afterwards of iron,
then termed mace, was principally used by the lower order, but
not always disdained by knights. In the Bayeux tapestry, a Norman
knight holds an iron club. Foot soldiers are there represented with
wooden clubs, which are thin at the lower end, and increase in
thickness towards the top. According to Guiart, quoted by Du
Cange, s. v. *Maxuca,* the common people of France were armed
with this weapon, which was also assigned to the plebeian body-guards
of princes. These guards were instituted by Richard I. and Philip
Augustus to protect them from the poignards of assassins. Their
services were not required in the battle field. The *Morgenstern,* or
spike-covered club, varied in its dimensions. According to Meyrick,
its staff was from two to five feet long, and the chain on which the
ball was suspended, even exceeded the length of five feet. The
balls, spiked or in the form of a channelled melon, weighed eight
pounds in some specimens. Single or triple chains connected the
balls with the handles. This weapon did not constitute a part of the
knightly armour. It was employed by German citizens and the
Switzers, and surpassed in size and weight the corresponding weapons
of other nations. The French probably became acquainted with it,
during the sieges of the cities of Flanders. The *Godendac* (good
day) derived its name from the dialect of the Flemings, and was
intended as a jocular allusion to the harsh welcome this species of club
gave to the French knights. Guiart speaks of it as a two-handed
cutting weapon. After the invention of gunpowder, it was gradually
rejected. In England, weapons of this kind were carried by the
pioneers of the Artillery Company, until the end of the last century.
Plate 14, Fig. 2, exhibits a Morning-star in the Dresden armory.
Plate 16, Fig. 6 represents a club in the shape of a flail. This
implement did great mischief in the wars of the Bohemians against
the Hussites.

Meyrick has given representations of knights holding small
single-handed instruments, which, instead of spikes, contained a
quantity of sharp knife-blades. The light club, Plate 14, Fig. 4,
was used at tournaments.

ANCIENT FIRE-ARMS.

Plates 14 *and* 15.

After the invention of gunpowder, no attention was given to the
manufacture of light fire-arms, but steady improvements   Heavy
were made in heavy artillery. Towards the end of the   Artillery.
fourteenth century, cannons were known and used in England,
France, Germany, and Spain. The manufacture of portable guns
does not appear to have commenced before the fifteenth century.
Vague conjectures have been made in reference to the use of the musket
in the war between the Venetians and the Genoese. Equally uncertain
are the statements which have been made with regard to portable
bombards and bombardelles.

Hand-cannons (*canons à main*) occur for the first time in 1411,
among the French. The army of John of Burgundy had
a supply of 4000 such cannons. Æneas Sylvius, without   Hand-cannons.
sufficient evidence, attributes the invention of this war-engine to the
Germans. It was in great favour in France and Italy, at the very
time it was employed in Germany against the Hussites. The
Florentines became acquainted with this weapon in 1432, and
introduced it at once among their troops. In 1449, the Milanese
armed their militia with no less than 20,000 muskets. The
introduction of these military implements, like the invention
of gunpowder, afforded no exclusive advantage to any particular state,
but became universally beneficial. The French, under Charles VIII.
being in possession of superior artillery, obtained a transient ascendancy
over the Italians, who, however soon became acquainted with the use
of these terrific engines. That secrecy which had been observed with
regard to the Greek fire, was no longer practicable in the application
of gunpowder.

In the earlier period of the middle ages, it had been the custom to
designate projecting engines by the names of certain birds. The
balista, for example, was called *Rebhuhn* (partridge). Another
engine bore the name of falcon, &c. After the invention of gunpowder,
this fashion of distinguishing the instruments of war by the familiar
names of living creatures, was applied to the engines which ejected
stone and metal bullets.

Muschet, according to Du Cange, is the name of the male hawk;
Muskets. the name of the fire-arm is therefore not to be derived from
Mouche (fly). A balista was known by that name even before
the invention of gunpowder, as is attested by Sanutus, in the
thirteenth century. The most ancient muskets were of considerable
bulk and weight. They differed from those represented in Plates
14 and 15. Being short, their range was not considerable. They
were fired by means of a match which came in contact with the
priming powder. As this process was inconvenient in taking aim, a
cock, in French *Serpentin,* was fixed to the right side of the musket.
The match was screwed into a hole at the top of the cock and thence
it came in contact with the priming. At the beginning of the
sixteenth century, these guns were already made longer and thinner.
About 1517, wheel locks, manufactured in Nuremberg, were known
in France, by the name of German locks. A wheel of steel being
moved by a spring, drew a spark from a stone screwed into the cock,
and communicated fire to the priming. The flints which were
used for that purpose being easily blunted, matchlocks, for a long
time, were preferred, though they were ineffectual in rainy weather,
and betrayed the troops to the enemy if attacks were made by night.

In the sixteenth century, long muskets were introduced. While
Long Muskets. being fired, their weight was supported by a fork-shaped
" *Rest,*" which, in German, was called *Bock,* and in French
Fourchette. The musketeers, when marching, carried the rests in their
right hands. Specimens of small arms are to be seen in Plates 14
and 15. Plate 14, Fig. 5, contains the delineation of a wheel lock, and
Plate 15, Fig. 1, that of a match lock. The former gun with a black
stock and inlaid with ivory or bone, is in the Dresden armory, and is
called the " Funeral musket," it having formerly been discharged at
the funerals of electors.

The soldiers carried their charges in bandoleers across their
shoulders. (Plate 14. Fig. 7). Powder flasks were usually carried
in hunting. Fig. 6 of the same plate represents the powder flask
of the musket, together with a key to wind up the wheel lock. The
metal powder flask is gilt, faced with velvet, and embellished with
black and yellow cords of silk.

HELMETS.

Plates 17, 18, 19, 20.

The head-covering, together with the shield, appear to have
composed the defensive arms of the ancient Germans. The
Helmets.
other portions of their armour were copied from the Romans.
Some passages in the works of Roman writers suggest that the ancient
Germans made little use of the helmet, or only adopted it from the
Romans, together with the body armour. Tacitus, in fact, affirms
that few Germans wore complete armour, and only in rare instances
were seen with helmets. Nevertheless, it is mentioned as a common
means of protection in the earliest traditions of the Scandinavians
who obviously came in no contact with the Romans or the Christian
Germans. The word helmet is of purely German origin; it is to be
found in the first written records of the victorious invaders of the
Roman empire, and was adopted from the German in the several
Romanesque languages.

The helmet is called in German *Helm,* in old French, *Healme* or
Hialm, subsequently, *Heaume* or *Hiaume,* in Italian, *Helmo* or *Elmo,*
in Spanish, *Yelmo.* Originally. the helmet appears to have been
nothing else but a leather cap, which did not descend below the
forehead. Such head coverings are represented in Anglo-Saxon
drawings of the tenth and eleventh centuries. Personages of a
superior rank had helmets of a conical form and gilt. After various
modifications, a small defensive projection was affixed to the helmet;
it descended to the nose, and was therefore, termed *Nasal.* Such
helmets continued in fashion in the tenth, eleventh, and even the
twelfth centuries. During the first crusade, the helmet with the
nasal protection appears to have been general, though in a painting
on glass of the 12th century, which is preserved in the Abbey of St.
Denis, and treats of the crusades, no notice is taken of it.

Visors were used by the heavy-armed cavalry of the Romans, but
were not at once adopted by the German tribes. Meyrick
refers the earliest specimen of a visor to the year 1155. Richard
Visors.
I. is pourtrayed in Meyrick's work with such a protection, which
consists of three horizontal bars. The helmet, hitherto conical,
received the form of a truncated cylinder. With such a helmet,

Richard I. is represented in his seal. In the seal, granted by Pope Eugene to the Templars, a knight is exhibited with a similarly-shaped helmet.

In addition to the helmet, knights wore other coverings on their heads. When chain-mail armour was the prevailing military costume of knights, a closely fitting cap of steel-rings was made in the same mode as the body armour. The cap of chain-mail (*capelline de maille*) inclosed the head as far as the forehead; the cheeks being left unprotected. The helmet rarely covered the ears, so that the mail cap could be seen from beneath the helmet. The latter was only put on when a knight was on the point of meeting the enemy, or of engaging in combat.

In the middle of the thirteenth century, the conical helmet came again into fashion. At top it was round, and sufficient space was left for a small skull-cap, to relieve the pressure of the heavy helmet. In the fourteenth and fifteenth centuries, this shape became very prevalent, and was retained until the seventeenth century, so long as the cuirassiers wore complete suits of armour. Plates of iron were fixed to the helmet with screws, or clasps and pins, to protect the neck and the throat, and thus replace the chain-mail. (See Plates 17 and 18). Visors were so commonly appended to the helmet, that no heavy-armed knight dispensed with them in combat. In the Assizes of Jerusalem the visored helmet (*heaume à visière*) is mentioned as a defensive piece of armour worn at duels. Visors considerably varied in form. They were furnished with face-guards (beavers) or small iron gratings, which could be raised or lowered at pleasure. The iron bars crossed each other at right angles. In some visors, three to four pieces were affixed perpendicularly or obliquely. In others, perforated plates were attached in lieu of bars. (See Plate 18). This fashion, shown also in Plates 33 and 48, does not seem to have been of rare occurrence. Meyrick represents the maid of Orleans with such a helmet, from a contemporaneous effigy at Orleans. The gorget was often connected with the tilting helmet, and fastened with rivets to the armour.

The bascinet was a lighter kind of head-covering. It was worn by Bascinets. squires, foot-soldiers, mercenaries, and even by heavy-armed horsemen and knights. These defensive coverings were called in French, *bacinets* or *cervelières*. They were used by knights who did not anticipate an immediate attack of the enemy, yet wished to be prepared for an emergency. They could be worn under the helmet like the hood of chain-mail. King Philip of Valois is represented by Meyrick with such a bascinet, the helmet being carried by one of his attendants. King Réné, in his Book of Tournaments, assigns similar head-coverings to the Germans. Heavy-armed knights of the fourteenth century wore visored bascinets instead of helmets. In Germany, bascinets were not used at tournaments. As a defensive armour of the infantry, they remained in use until the latter half of the seventeenth century. Additional security was afforded by projecting beaks in the front and back of this head-dress, which sometimes terminated in a spike or was adorned with a crest. In some instances the helmets were supplied with ear-pieces or bands, which were covered with small metal scales, and fastened below the chin. Helmets, at an early period, were enriched with ornaments. We have already noticed the nasal piece which was embellished with the figure of a lion. In Anglo-Saxon miniatures, the nobles wear their helmets overlaid with gold, and set with jewels. Of great antiquity, was the fashion among Kings and Dukes, to encircle their helmets with crowns or diadems, as is seen in the seal of Edward the Confessor. Also in the miniature of Philip of Valois, the bascinet of that king is adorned with the crown of France. Gilding was much in vogue. In the thirteenth and fourteenth centuries, horse-tails were not unfrequently used in ornamenting the helmets. These embellishments were subsequently supplanted by plumes of feathers. Meyrick is of opinion that this ornament of the helmet was not common before the fifteenth century. It was then only that the pompous display of plumes came into fashion. Rich knights were not always contented with a single bunch of feathers. Three rows were often circularly arranged one above the other. The plumage was either raised vertically, or drooped towards the sides of the helmet. Montfaucon has given the figure of a knight, whose plumes proceed from a tube at the top of the helmet, and sweep down like a fox-tail, almost touching the back of the horse.

Other ornaments of the helmet consisted of foliage, heads of animals, horns, &c. In war, such embellishments were objectionable, on account of the advantages they afforded to the adversary. On coming to close quarters, these projections served as handles, by which the wearer was dragged down and unhorsed. Owing to such dangerous superadditions, Stephen, King of England, fell into the hands of his enemies. It is possible that feathers came into general favour after the invention of gunpowder, when hand to hand fights were of shorter duration and proved less decisive than they had been previously, namely, before the middle of the fifteenth century. At tournaments, figures of animals and other objects were used for decorative purposes. Richard I. is represented on his seal, as wearing on this cylindrical helmet, the broom-plant (*genesta*), from which his house derived the name of Plantagenet (*planta genestæ*, or *genistæ*). Meyrick dates this fashion of ornamenting the helmets from the reign of Edward III. In the middle of the fifteenth century, these decorations were so common that King Réné, in his *Livre des Tournois*, considers them as indispensable. Ornamental crests were made hereditary, like armorial bearings. After Plate 35, several ornamented tilting helmets may be seen.

Helmets shaped in imitation of the heads of animals belong to the ostentatious eccentricities of the later middle ages. (See Plate 19, Fig. 5).

BODY ARMOUR.

Plates 20, 21, 22, 23, 24.

Body Armour. It has been noticed that the Germans became acquainted with body armour on coming in contact with the heavy cavalry of the Romans. It may not be out of place to offer a brief notice of the armour worn by the Romans, at the dissolution of the empire, and imitated by the Germans. The principal authority on this subject is Ammianus Marcellinus. The horsemen were sheathed in iron. The limbs were protected by small overlapping and movable metal scales. The helmet protected the face so securely, that missiles could only pass through the apertures left for the sight and for breathing. The horsemen were termed *cataphracti* (*i.e*, men armed *cap-a-pie*), and formed at the time of Constantine, a considerable part of the army. Vegetius gives no description of their armour, and only states that in single combat, the riders, though protected from injury, could easily be taken prisoners, on account of their ponderous armour; but when concentrated in masses, they did good service, and often broke through the ranks of the enemy. In another passage, this author observes that the barbarians gained their victories by the adoption of the Roman defensive armour which, probably, included both the breast-plate of the legionary soldier, and the complete suit of the equestrian warrior. The body armour was covered with small movable metal scales, or with rings twisted within one another. Also, the horses were covered with housings of metal scales.

Cuirass and Hauberk. The names of the several defensive pieces of the arms and legs, are not derived from the language of the Germans. The German word *Kürass* (in English, *cuirass*, in French *cuirasse*, in Italian, *corazo*, in Spanish, *coraza*) is derived from the Latin *corium*, leather, for it was during the decline of the Roman power, and the decrease of discipline among the legionary soldiers, that the heavy breast-plates were replaced by leather defences; these, being lighter, were commonly worn after the reign of Constantine the Great. The German word *Panzer* is derived from the vulgar Latin term *pansa*, (in English, *paunch*), indicating that it was a safeguard of the body.

The terms *Harnisch* and *Halsberg*, which relate to body armour, are of German origin. *Harnisch* is derived from the old German word, *isarn*, *iârn*, or *hiârn*, and signifies wrought iron. This word is represented in English by *hurness*, in French and Spanish by the terms of *harnois* and *arnes*, and in Italian, by *arnese*. The signification of *Halsberg*, (in French, *halberg* and *hauberc*, and in English *hauberk*) was in the course of time restricted to chain-mail armour. It is said to be derived from *al*, (all) and *bergen*, (to shelter).

We have no monumental evidence as to the construction of German armour at the conquest of the Roman empire; though ample proofs exist that the Goths, Franks, and other German tribes were acquainted with that defensive habiliment. Clovis, for example, in the battle against the Visigoths, saved his life by his cuirass. In the earliest specimens, the harness is composed of overlapping scales. The portrait of Charlemagne is thus represented by Montfaucon from a contemporary mosaic. Eginhard, who states that Charlemagne wore armour, makes use of the Roman word *thorax*, (breast-plate). The Anglo-Saxon king Hengist wore scale-armour in battle.

It is probable that iron armour was not the common wear of combatants, and that only the superior vassals of the crown, (mentioned under the name of *Caballarii*, in Charlemagne's Capitularies), were required to come to battle completely accoutred. These defences did not cover the whole body, but only descended to the hip, or came down to the knees like a tunic. The illustration given in Plate 20 is copied from a specimen which is preserved in Dresden, and once belonged to John Sobiesky, king of Poland. It differs, in various details, from the most ancient form; the helmet, for example, being adorned with feathers, and having cheek pieces. The metal scales are fastened on a leather lining. In the 10th century, armour composed of rings came into fashion. It is exhibited in Anglo-Saxon miniatures, and probably distinguished the opulent class of nobles. Such a dress reached to the hips (Plate 24); but in the 11th century, it was made to join the knees, hanging down loosely like a tunic, or being made in the shape of breeches. In this fashion, the Norman knights of William the Conqueror are represented in the Bayeux tapestry. This armour, which in German is termed *Halsberg*, (hauberc) contains breeches (*bainberc* or *chausses de fer*), together with a hood, which closed round the head and neck. The whole garment looked as if made of a single piece. The knight, while dressing himself with it, first put on the *chausses*, then passed the arms through the sleeves, and at last drew the hood over the head. The covering of the legs below the knees, as also of the feet, was made of leather. The rings were not linked together, but were set edge-wise on a garment of leather, or of a quilted material. Such armour was often composed of small pins, four or eight of which were turned downwards, and a corresponding number was fastened obliquely, exhibiting a chequered surface.

At the first crusade, knights were, in all probability, equipped in the manner just described, but in the twelfth century, the Chain-mail. body armour was so constructed that the rings, instead of being set edge-wise, were linked together in the form of a chain. Four rings were attached to a fifth. This process was probably

of eastern invention, and as it allowed the garment to be extremely pliable, it was eagerly adopted by the Europeans. Some Asiatic nations wear such armour to the present day. The most ancient relic of this kind Meyrick assigns to the reign of Henry II. Such a hauberk often consisted of double rings, and, for the sake of comfort, hung loosely round the body. In the thirteenth century, this armour appears to have been made of two separate pieces; namely, of a coat with hood, and of a covering for the legs. The coat reached to the knees like a tunic, and the housings came down to the feet; these afterwards were also screened by an interlaced covering. Plate 24 illustrates this fashion, which seems to have been favoured by princes and wealthy nobles. A quilted garment was worn beneath the hauberk, which sometimes protruded from the ends of the armour. Its German name *Wamms* was adopted in the Romanesque languages (in French *Wambaison or Gambaison*, in Spanish, *Guambason*, in English *Gambeson*). It joined the hips, and was furnished with sleeves. According to Du Cange, (s. v. *gambiso*) it was stuffed with cotton or wool. This defensive garment was of greater antiquity than the chain-mail hauberk, it having been worn by Charlemagne, as is attested by Eginhard.

Horses were likewise covered with chain-mail armour. A chronicler, describing the crusades of the Emperor Frederic I., calls Horse Armour. the Germans an iron people riding on iron horses. The Crusaders, who, in 1204, took Constantinople, are said to have fought on horses covered with mail-housings. The Greeks were as much terrified by the horses as at the sight of their apparently invulnerable riders. Godfrey of Bouillon's Assizes of Jerusalem direct that knights, challenged to single combat, should appear on barbed horses. The housings of chain-mail for the protection of the flanks and legs of the horses could be made of any length the knight desired. The head of the horse was to be armed with an iron-spiked plate. (See Plate 30 and several of the succeeding illustrations).

Chain-mail gradually gave way to plate armour, large portions of which consisted of one or several pieces, and had movable Mixed Armour. joints; the plates being adapted to the several limbs. Large metal plates were originally attached to the elbows, knees, and feet, and afterwards also to the arms and legs; ultimately, the breast and body were likewise covered with them. During the greater part of the fourteenth century, mixed armour was preferred. Copies from ancient monuments frequently show metal plates for the legs, and chain-mail for the arms. Sometimes, the reverse was the case, and chain-mail was employed for the protection of the body.

Thus equipped, the English and French fought in the wars which Edward III. waged for the recovery of the French crown. The monumental figure of Bernabo Visconti at Milan, (of 1365) appears similarly armed. At the end of the fourteenth century, a species of armour came into fashion, in which the breast was protected by a single metal plate, or by several bands of more or less width, which were arranged in parallel lines. The protecting pieces of the arms, legs, and waist were also composed of such bands. Gradually, these pieces were replaced by single plates. This species of armour was evidently preferred to chain-mail, for being impervious to the edge of the sword or the point of the lance; as both weapons glided off more easily from the polished iron plate, than from chain-mail, the surface of which afforded more scope to the assaults of the antagonist. After the invention of gunpowder, plate-armour came into favour, owing to its greater safety. Meyrick states that plate-covered coats were more convenient than coats of chain-mail, which were worn on the padded gambeson. Coats of chain-mail were not given up altogether even as late as the sixteenth century, and were worn beneath the plate-armour, from the borders of which they occasionally protruded. In the adjoining illustrations, several specimens of this description will be found. Plate-armour continued to be worn by the heavy cavalry to the end of the seventeenth century. It was then reduced to that size of the breast-plate, which is still used by the cuirassiers of the present time.

When the breast-plate came into general use, a hook, termed lance-rest, was attached to the right side for supporting the Lance-rests. lance in the charge. This rest is to be noticed in most specimens of the fifteenth century, but in some instances, it was replaced by a lengthy, horizontal, and slighty concave iron bar. Chain-mail for the protection of horses was, as early as the fifteenth century, superseded by plate-armour. An example of this equipment is offered in Plate 47.

The body armour, as has been noticed, was often covered with large iron bands joined together in parallel lines. Sometimes, the surface was made up of small lozenge-shaped plates of iron. This kind was still used in the first half of the fifteenth century, but since then, it was discontinued. Representations of such armour are given in Plate 21, and in several specimens after Plate 29.

Besides the body armour as depicted in Plates 20, 24, and 35, &c., illustrations are offered of different shapes, which came into fashion after the end of the fourteenth century. Plate 20, Fig. 2, is copied from a specimen in the Dresden armory. Plate 21 exhibits the armour of Joachim II., Elector of Brandenburg. This specimen, together with Plate 22, Fig. 1, and Plate 23, Fig. 1 and 2, are copied from Schrenk's copper-plates.

We have already noticed that after the introduction of plate-armour, the art of defensive warfare became superior to the art of destruction, especially in close attack. The ancient weapons were less hurtful when directed against solid and polished armour, than against pliable chain-mail. The bolts, discharged from the cross-bow, recoiled ineffectually from the smooth plates, which resisted, in a great measure, the assaults of the sword, the lance, and the spiked club.

This superiority in the art of defence, which appeared to add to influence of the nobles, was, however, of brief duration. Plate-armour inefficient. Some tens of years after the introduction of plate-armour, the power of cavalry gave way to the effect of musketry and to the force of heavy ordnance; after a few centuries, this cavalry proved so utterly incapable of resisting fire-arms, that the defensive coverings were given up or reduced to the mere size of the breast-plate. Nor must it be imagined that a complete armour ever made a warrior invincible. In actual battle, it entailed many disadvantages, which turned the scale in favour of light-armed infantry. The weight of the harness paralysed the physical strength of the combatant. At the slightest confusion, rapid evolutions became totally impracticable. We have already stated that the English foot-soldiers owed their triumph at the battle of Agincourt to their superior agility. The French knights also suffered severely from the attacks of the civic troops of Flanders. The former required too much time for the adjustment of their armour, and were, in consequence of this circumstance, defeated by their enemies. For the same reason, an ascendancy was gained by the Swiss foot-soldiers over the Austrian nobles, and by the German towns-men over the inconveniently-armed aristocracy. Lastly, we must not lose sight of the many casualties and discomforts to which the heavy-armed horsemen were exposed.

The heat of summer made the armour insupportable, and exposed the wearer to the dangers of suffocation and apoplexy, or produced, at least, such a debility as to disable him from wielding his weapons. In fording rivers or passing over marshy ground, the weight of the accoutrement tended to imperil life. Moreover, it was scarcely possible to coerce an antagonist to fight; the slightest impediment, and any insignificant entrenchment being sufficient to baffle the attack of the unwieldy assailants or to throw them into disorder. Difficulties like these account for the abolition of heavy armour in the time of Louis XIV., when the art of warfare assumed a new and improved character.

GAUNTLETS, SHIELDS, SADDLES, SPURS, AND HERALDIC COAT-ARMOUR.

Plates 25, 26, 27, 28, *et seq.*

The great antiquity of the glove or gauntlet may be conjectured from the frequent symbolical use of this covering, and from its uniform occurrence among the several Germanic tribes.

Gauntlets.

The word gauntlet, in French *gant*, in Italian *guanto*, in Spanish *guante*, in Old German, *want*, in mediæval Latin, *wantus*, may be traced to the German word *hand*. Like the helmet, the gauntlet is mentioned in old Scandinavian literature. Gloves were originally made of leather, but when mail armour came into fashion, the gloves were likewise covered with interlaced rings, which were superseded by metal plates. Guiard mentions the gauntlet, or plate-covered gloves between the years 1296 and 1314, and Meyrick refers the most ancient monumental specimen of this kind to the year 1298. Guiard also speaks of *gans de baleine*, or gloves covered with whale-bone. Towards the end of the fourteenth century, a large plate, attached to the glove, protected the lower part of the arm. The hands and fingers were guarded by small overlapping plates. Coverings of this description continued to be worn until the 17th century.

The gloves were used for several symbolical purposes, of which we enumerate the following :—

I. By tendering or throwing the glove, the Franks, Longobards, Alemanni, and Saxons indicated the conveyance of property, or the transfer of privileges. This custom was observed for a long time. Conradin, when about to be executed, threw his glove into the air, that it might be seen by those who attended his execution. By this act, he resigned his territorial rights in favour of his kinsman, Peter of Aragon.

Gloves used as Symbols.

II. The glove thrown down by sovereigns or judges served as a sign that a criminal under trial forfeited his estates. In this manner, the Emperor Frederic I. pronounced sentence upon the Italian cities.

III. The throwing down of the gauntlet was notoriously equivalent to a challenge. If taken up by the adversary, it was understood that the challenge was accepted. The gauntlet was sometimes thrown into the face of the defendant. Its removal from the hand most likely implied that the appellant had withdrawn his friendship from the defendant. In trials by wager of battle, the presiding judge took charge of the gloves of both parties.

IV. The glove indicated the authority conferred upon subalterns by their superiors. Monarchs used to despatch messengers who were the bearers of such gloves. A German emperor, for example, sent a glove to cities on which he conferred the right of holding markets.

V. Gloves, set with pearls and precious stones, formed part of the crown insignia of the German empire, and were considered as symbols of the Emperor's authority.

The shield is one of the most ancient and most common military implement of the Germans. Its name is of German origin, and occurs in all the languages derived from the Latin. It is called in Old French *Escu*, in Italian *Scudo*, in Spanish *Escudo*, etc. Though all these words might be derived from the Latin *Scutum*, they more likely sprang from the Germanic word *Skild, or Skiold*. The shield was also known by the German name of *Tartsche*, (in Old French *Targe*, and in English *Target*).

Shields.

The original shape of the shield cannot be ascertained. It was probably of sufficient size to protect the whole body. Among the Anglo-Saxons of the ninth and tenth centuries, its shape was oval. The frame was encircled by a stout iron band, and had an *umbo* or boss (a sharp iron spike) in the centre. The remaining portion of the shield consisted of wood covered with leather. The shield of the Franks was triangular, wide at the top, and pointed below. This shape came into general fashion, and was, throughout the middle ages, in favor among the members of chivalry. On the Bayeux tapestry, Norman knights are represented with such shields. Some of these defensive instruments are there represented as round in the upper part. (See Plates 35 and 36). In some instances, the shields were made convex. According to Meyrick, they were four feet long, but this length probably varied. In the fifteenth century, the size was altered. The shields were made shorter and square. At the top and the bottom, they were bent forward in obtuse angles. With a shield of this kind, Henry VI. is pourtrayed in Meyrick's work. After the reign of that king, shields ceased to be used in battle. The shield of knights was either covered with a sheet of iron, or consisted of a thin metal plate. When not required in actual combat, it was carried by a strap over the shoulder, as may be seen in Plates 35 and 36. These two forms were of most frequent occurrence, but those of a round shape, as in Plates 26 and 27, were likewise in use. Iron spikes fixed to shields were sometimes used in assault, (see the same Plates). The Assizes of Jerusalem required of the knight armed for the duel, that his shield should have two iron spikes in front, one in the centre and the other below; their thickness was optional, but in length, they were not to exceed a foot. The shield might be surrounded by an indefinite number of spikes. Specimens are exhibited in Plates 27 and 57. Plate 26, Fig. 4, represents the pavise carried by a special bearer for the protection of a crossbow-man. Fig. 1 is a large shield for foot-soldiers. Such shields were used by the Bohemians as late as the middle of the 16th century.

The embellishments of the shield are of an earlier date than those of the other weapons. Even Tacitus noticed that the Germans ornamented their shields with choice colours. Painted shields are to be seen in the most ancient monuments, before armorial bearings were in fashion. In the Bayeux tapestry, for example, the shields of Norman knights are adorned with emblematic figures, such as crosses, dragons, etc., which, however, are in no connection with the charges in an escutcheon. Armorial bearings were, according to Meyrick, introduced in the latter half of the twelfth century. Also among the other nations of Western Europe, shields were at this date painted with the arms of their noble owners. Shields were hung up in sepulchral vaults. If a noble family became extinct, the shield was dashed to pieces, and thrown into the grave of the last of the lineage.

Ornamented Shields.

Among the ancient Germans, the shield was employed for certain symbolical observances. A king, whether called to the throne by election or by the right of succession, was seated on an elevated shield, and thrice carried about within the circle of the assembled people, by whom he was hailed with shouts and clapping of hands. This solemnity, which is even recorded by Tacitus, is interpreted by Grimm, as a symbol of the people's concurrence and sanction. This custom was practised by the Lombards, Goths, and Franks, but not by the Scandinavians. Paulus Diaconus alludes to this ceremony in reference to the Lombard King Agilulf. Among the Goths, Vitiges announced his election by declaring that he had assumed his royal dignity by the raising of shields, according to ancestral usage. With respect to the Franks, Gregory of Tours treats of this custom in referring to Clovis, Sigibert, and Gundobald. Also, Pepin was thus exhibited to the people, in 752, after having been crowned and anointed. This ancient custom was abolished in the time of the German Emperors, though it was still remembered in popular traditions. The *Heldenbuch*, (*i.e.*, the Heroes' Book) relates, that Hugdietrich was made king by the raising of shields. Once more, and for the last time, this custom was revived in 1204, when the Crusaders of France, Flanders, and Venice, conquered Constantinople and chose Baldwin as Latin Emperor. After the election, the new Emperor was elevated on a shield, and even one of his competitors assisted in carrying the Emperor elect to the church of St. Sophia.

Symbols.

The spurs are, by their very names, proved to be of German origin. Their name has passed into all the Romanesque languages. It is in old French *esperon*, in modern French *éperon*, in Spanish *espolon* or *espuela*, and in mediæval Latin, *spourones*. Ancient spurs belonging to a son of Pepin are mentioned by Du Cange. Anglo-Saxon spurs of the tenth and eleventh centuries were furnished with a single goad. This form is the most ancient; it is exhibited in the Bayeux tapestry with a single spike, and is slightly hollow at both sides. Monuments of that period exhibit the goad

Spurs.

of the spur in the shape of a lance. In the fourteenth century, a spiked, movable wheel (a rowel) replaced the former single point. The rod on which the goad, and afterwards the rowel, was fixed, was originally straight, but since the fourteenth century, curved as at present.

Gilt spurs, being a sign of chivalry, were denied to men of inferior rank. Nobles who were not knighted, were only permitted to wear silver spurs. If a man was degraded from the rank of knighthood, he was deprived of his spurs.

Saddles. Saddles are first mentioned by Sidonius Apollinaris in reference to the Visigoths. Those of the Anglo-Saxons merely consisted of a pillow. In the eleventh century, large projections were added in front and behind, for the convenience of heavy-armed knights. This form, which is represented in the Bayeux tapestry, prevailed throughout the middle ages. (See Plate 28, Fig. 1, etc.) The saddle there depicted is in the Dresden armoury. The style of its embellishments suggests that it belonged to the fifteenth or sixteenth century. The covering consists of black velvet richly embroidered with gold. The spurs, in that plate, are copied from an example, in the same collection. Fig. 3 exhibits a specimen of spurs enriched with garnets and other jewels. Among the Germanic tribes, the act of placing a saddle upon a man was a curious mode of inflicting a degrading punishment. In the German empire, commoners and those nobles who were tenants of others, were liable to carry this badge of disgrace. Among the French, rulers and princes were even not exempt from this punishment. This kind of humiliation implied that the offender appeared in the category of beasts of burden.

Surcoats. As a part of the chivalric equipment, we mention the surcoat, or coat of arms (*Wapenrock*), a garment which was made of fine wool, silk, and other costly materials. It was worn over the armour, and ornamented, in the thirteenth century, with embroidered emblazonments. The caparisons of the horses were often decorated in a style corresponding with the upper garments of the knights. Fashion made this species of dress very variable. The illustrations introduced after Plate 39 are of the fifteenth century.

TOURNAMENTS.

Those martial sports of the middle ages which a famous historian considers superior to the gymnastic games of the classical period, may fairly be traced back to the earliest stage Tournaments. of German antiquities, and were the natural amusements of a warlike people. Tacitus speaks of a dance of arms among the Germans, and Cassiodorus makes mention in several places of warlike performances that took place at the annual musters of the Goths. Also, Nithard mentions a mock fight, which was fought between the troops of Louis of Germany and those of Charles the Bald, before an immense concourse of the people, and in which the two princes, with their retinue, took an active part. The Anglo-Saxons engaged at public festivals, in similar sports, with shields and clubs. Such pastimes remained in practice even after the Norman invasion, until the twelfth century. Military games, in so far as they were subject to certain regulations and universal customs, owed their progress to the establishment of heavy cavalry among the feudal nobility and chivalry. The introduction of tournaments in Germany is assigned by chroniclers to the reign of Henry I. In France, the origin of these games was attributed to Gaufroy de Preuilly, a knight who died in 1066. Whether these dates are correct or not, there is no doubt that chivalric games were in great favour at the beginning of the twelfth century. The laws and customs peculiar to these tournaments were then fully developed, and remained in force until the dawn of the modern era. As regards the institution of tournaments in England, we possess more exact information; they were first undertaken by the Norman knights during the reign of King Stephen. Henry II. prohibited these sports, but Richard I., famed for his dexterity in the use of arms, cultivated them with passionate fondness. He understood, at the same time, how to derive a revenue from them, by exacting heavy taxes for the permission of holding a tournament. An earl had to pay for such a permission, twenty marks of silver, a baron, ten marks, and a knight, four. It is uncertain when the displays of the tournament came into fashion among the Italians, the Spaniards, and the Scandinavians. The latter, most likely, became acquainted with them through the Germans. It is very probable, that the tournaments in Scandinavia dated from the twelfth or thirteenth century; and that in Spain and

Italy, they were contemporaneous with those held in France and Germany. After the fourteenth century, tournaments were even held by the Byzantines and the Moors in Spain. With these exercises, the latter combined the hurling of the javelin, a practice which was not in use among the other nations of Western Europe.

The word tournament (in German *turnier*, in French *tournoi*, in Spanish *torneo*, &c.) is of German origin and designates Meaning of Tournament. bodily exercises in general. Another German word, *Buhurd*, which means a mock fight, between troops of combatants, occurs also in French (*Bohord*). Independently of historical testimony, the very fact, that those words are derived from the German, is in itself, an evidence that the early Germans were the originators of such martial sports.

In tournaments, the grandest spectacles of the middle ages, the Interest in Tournaments. aristocracy had an opportunity of displaying their rich and glittering pageantry, as well as their skill in arms. The passion for such diversions was natural at a time, when no other popular sports of equal magnitude were known. They who joined in the chivalric games could indulge in their love of glory, or rather, in the vanity of exhibiting their wealth and their warlike prowess. Courage was required even in a mock battle. Although, during the sport, the combatants renounced their personal or national antipathies; although the weapons were blunt, and it was unlawful to injure the unprotected parts of the body, it nevertheless occasionally happened, that mock fights ended in deaths or dangerous wounds. It was nearly as great an honour to be successful in a tournament as to gain a victory in real warfare. Indeed, the prowess displayed in the joust, must have produced, for the moment, greater sensation than exploits in the field, which are unattended by the applause of admiring witnesses. The spectators consisted not merely of the wondering multitude, but of princes, and chief of all, of ladies, who awarded honours and distinctions. In vain did the popes exert their authority to abolish these perilous sports. Their interference proved as ineffectual in this instance as in the attempt of limiting the use of offensive weapons. Tournaments were not merely interesting for their festivities and merry entertainments, but also for affording to the meetings of nobles an eligible opportunity of fixing or deliberating upon military or political undertakings. As the result of such an

assemblage, we may instance the crusade suggested by Fulco of Neuilly, which led to the conquest of Constantinople. The Crusaders, consisting of the knights of France and Flanders, were enlisted in the enterprize, both by taking part in the tournaments, and by listening to exciting sermons preached at the festivals of the church. The mock fights of the tourney were alike among nearly all the western nations, though we are not aware of the existence of a common code of laws, relative to tournaments, anterior to the beginning of the fifteenth century. It was then that the first complete work on the regulations of tournaments was composed by King Réné. It is entitled *Les Tournois du Roi Réné*, and was edited by Champollion in 1829. The description we here offer of tournaments is chiefly derived from that work.

A tournament could only be proclaimed by a prince, a high baron, or a banneret. In Germany, the knights of the empire Proclamation (of Franconia, Suabia, Bavaria, and the Rhine), were of a Tournament. authorised to proclaim tournaments. The whole festivity had the appearance of a combat, and assumed this character at the onset, the announcement being made in the shape of a challenge. He who proposed the tournament, despatched a herald with a tilting sword, which was delivered to the party challenged. The terms of *Appellant* and *Defendant* were applied to the knights who took the lead of the contending parties. The tourney being accepted by the defendant, he had to select four judges, (*juges diseurs*) out of a list of eight knights and four squires. He had also to present the herald-at-arms with a costly garment, embroidered with gold or made of scarlet satin. The herald received a large sheet of parchment, containing the effigies of the appellant and defendant, who were pourtrayed in the act of tourneying; the four corners contained the armorial bearings of the judges. The herald, placing this picture on his shoulders, and being followed by his poursuivants (*poursuivans d'armes*) appeared with his authorisation before the judges, who determined at what time and place the military festival should be celebrated. The intended sport was now publicly announced by the herald, and parchment rolls, with the armorial devices of the judges, were distributed among the bystanders. The judges had authority to decide in which places the tournament should be proclaimed, but in no case could they omit the court of the sovereign.

The ordinary weapons of assault at these chivalric games, consisted **Tourneying Weapons.** of a lance, a bâton, (or club) and a sword. The lance terminated in a cronel or coronel, *i.e.*, a small crown. In the fifteenth century, the grasp of the lance was furnished with the vamplate, or small guard for the protection of the hand. This guard was called, in German, *Schwebeisen* or *Gärbeisen*. According to King Réné, the blade was to be four inches broad, and one inch thick at the side of the edge, lest it might penetrate the visor of the helmet. It varied in length. Réné states that both the sword and the club should not exceed the length of the arm. (See Plate 32). Instead of the cross-bar of the sword, the hilt was, for the sake of greater safety, guarded by a ring. Réné suggests that the sword and club should be fastened by means of a chain or a cord to the arm or the belt, to obviate the necessity of dismounting, in the event of the weapons being dropped. The swords and clubs were examined a day before the tournament. If the weapons had the due length and weight, and were approved, a stamp was impressed on them.

The defensive armour of the French, English, and other nations, **Defensive Armour.** was lighter than that of the Germans. Besides various defensive pieces of metal, the non-German knights wore cuirasses, like those worn by foot-soldiers. Beneath the armour, they had the *Gambeson* or *Wambais*, (in German *Wamms*) which was padded in the shoulders, arms, and the back; the attack being principally directed against these parts. The Germans, in the fifteenth century, gave their preference to stouter and heavier armour. At the same time, their under-garments were thickly quilted in the chest, as also in the body, and moreover, stuffed with cotton. This precaution enabled the warriors to fight with more safety, but deprived their movements of the necessary ease. The bascinet is mentioned by Réné as the head covering of the French. The ornamental part of the helmet, lined with leather, was fastened on this bascinet. The Germans, however, wore large heavy helmets, proportioned to the stout body-armour. The decorations of the helmet, like the insignia on the horse-trappings and the coat-of-arms, served as badges or signs, by which the combatants could be recognised during the sport. The helmet, while suspended on the pommel of the saddle, was attached by a small chain to the covering of the breast, to secure it from slipping down.

The flanks of the horses were guarded by bands of straw, which were drawn together with strings and attached to the **Horse-Armour** pommel. As these defensive appliances must impede the movements of the animal, they were fastened on wooden staves. A crescent-shaped bag, stuffed with straw, protected the breast of the war-horse. The projecting bands of straw were covered with trappings which generally bore the heraldic devices of the knights. (See Plate 33). The adoption of horse-armour was designed with a view of protecting the horses from violent collisions, and of securing the legs of the riders from contusions. At the *Behords*, or tournaments in which combatants met in large numbers, these coverings were important means of defence.

The judges of the combat appointed the time and place of the encounter, and superintended the erection of the lists. **Erection of the Lists.** The plain inclosed was an oblong, the length exceeding the breadth by one fourth. The platforms for the judges and the ladies occupied one side of the arena. The other sides were left to the common spectators. The barriers were erected in double lines. Each barrier consisted of two beams, which were placed horizontally and in parallel lines. The lower beam reached to the knees. Between this double barrier, a space of four steps was left for the attendants, who had to keep off the crowd.

Four days before the festivity, both the appellant and defendant were required to make their appearance with their suite **Arrival of the Tourneyers.** of combatants, servants, and trumpeters. After making a circuit round the place of the tourney, they and their companions exhibited their armorial devices and crests in the windows of their residences. Then the four judges and the king-at-arms with his poursuivants, made their entry in state. The judges were attired in long richly-flowing garments; as signs of office, they carried long white staves, with which they appeared in public, during the whole term of the festivity. On their arrival, the leaders placed under their jurisdiction the stewards, the paymasters of the tournament, and the other officers. They now undertook the direction of the whole festivity, and superintended the entertainments. The king-at-arms was stationed before their residence as a guard of honour, holding their four banners in his hand. The tourneyers were bound to submit to the scrutiny of the judges, their armorial ensigns, crests, etc. As soon as they had arrived, the festivity was opened with a banquet and a ball. On the next day, the judges had to enquire into the character of the knights who wished to join the tournament. Ladies and other personages of distinction, who desired to witness the tournament, were then admitted. Helmets and armorial bearings were arranged in lines, and a herald proclaimed the names of the respective owners. Objections against individual combatants were indicated by a touch of the helmets, which were then turned down by the squires or poursuivants, and on the next day, the questionable cases were referred to the discretion of the judges. Noblemen, guilty of heinous offences, were excluded from the tourney. Admission was refused to nobles who were accused of a breach of promise, of lending money on usury, of having married the daughter of a plebeian, or of producing an unsatisfactory pedigree. The excluded individual received, a day before the combat, due notice to withdraw. If he defied the order, he was beaten by the tourneying knights until he abandoned his horse; the attendants then cut asunder the strap of his saddle. The delinquent had to sit astride on the barriers, and be watched, lest he should leap down, or throw himself on the ground. In this attitude, he was compelled to witness the conclusion of the tournament. His horse became the perquisite of the poursuivants. If a nobleman had married a plebeian woman, the bridle of his horse was rent asunder, his emblazonments were flung to the ground, and he was kept in custody at the barriers. A nobleman with an imperfect pedigree, could only be admitted into the lists, if princes or personages of high rank touched him with their swords or clubs. In that case, he was permitted to take part in all the tournaments, and improve his crest. If a nobleman had injured the reputation of a lady, and had been convicted of slander, he was flogged until he invoked the compassion of the lady he had defamed.

On the second day, the two leaders, with their retainers, had to enter the lists, and to take the oath of the tournament, in the presence of the judges. The knights were then richly attired, and carried hurtless lances. The banners were kept furled. The judges now administered the oath to the nobles, by which they were pledged to abstain from striking a man below the belt, from attacking anyone who was unhelmed, or from inflicting unfair blows; they were, in fact, rigidly bound to observe the directions of the judges.

King Réné, who cites the oath of the tournament, adds to the formula, that the transgressing combatants should lose their horses and weapons, and be for ever excluded from the lists. These regulations were enforced in France and in Germany. In England, knights and squires who infringed the rules of combat were liable to an imprisonment of from one to three years, besides the forfeiture of their horses.

The judges of the tournament had now to nominate the knight of honour (*chevalier d'honneur, Ehrenherold*), who acted as the representative of the fair sex. Two ladies, distinguished for beauty and rank, were conducted by the judges to this officiating knight, and delivered to him the head-gear of a lady. During the performance of the joust, the knight of honour carried this head-dress on a lance. If one of the combatants was in jeopardy, and the ladies ordered their representative to lower his lance, no tourneyer was permitted to continue the attack; hence this head-dress was termed "the Mercy of the Ladies," (*la Mercy des Dames*).

The real tournament commenced on the third day. The platform assigned to the ladies being filled, the judges, together with the knight of honour, made their appearance; the *The Day of the Tournament.* latter being dressed in full armour, and holding the sign of office at the top of his lance. They rode round the lists to inspect the preparations for the combat, and to give the necessary directions to the several attendants. A space in the middle of the lists being parted off by cords, the tourneyers were expected to stand at opposite sides. The knight of honour rode into the central space, being accompanied by the judges, who removed the helmet from his head, and put it on a lance, which was fixed into the ground, before the platform of the ladies. The knight of honour remained with his followers within that barrier, until all the combatants had arrived. The judges, meanwhile, withdrew to their platform. King Réné suggests to the tourneyers that they should perfectly rest themselves the night previous to the combat, since they must be exclusively occupied with their armour after ten in the morning, and appear at one o'clock fully accoutred and mounted before the residence of their leader. Each cavalier was allowed to bring with him servants on foot and on horseback. A prince might bring four mounted attendants, a count three, a knight two, a squire one. The number of foot-attendants was not limited.

As soon as the tourneyers had assembled in the lists, the challenger, with his followers, entered on horseback. Both parties stopped at the cords, which divided the lists, and drew up in array of battle. The standard-bearers were stationed by the side of their masters. The mounted attendants took their position close behind them with light body armour, helmets, and shafts of lances. The foot-attendants, also, occupied their posts. The heralds and trumpeters were placed in the intermediate space of the divided lists. The two parties now shouted the battle-cry, brandishing their swords and clubs at each other. The king-at-arms once more proclaimed the laws of the tournament, and, conformably to the directions of the judges, he thrice repeated the order that the cords should be cut asunder. The standard-bearers called out the *mot de guerre* of their masters, the trumpeters sounded their instruments, and the combat began.

These regulations evidently related to those tournaments in which many mounted champions were engaged. Conflicts of foot-warriors or of mixed combatants, likewise took place at such contests, as for instance, the storming of castles, or the defence of bridges. If, by any mishap, a champion was thrown down, it was the duty of the attendants to carry him to a place of safety, or to raise him up again, but if the crowd prevented them from rendering the necessary assistance, they had to gather around him, ward off the strokes aimed at him, and protect him from being injured by the hoofs of the horses. Tumultuous conflicts were checked by the interference, or, as it was termed, the Mercy of the Ladies. To these regulations, others were added with a view of mitigating the dangers of the encounter. It was not lawful for two combatants simultaneously to attack a single adversary. Any one was at liberty to withdraw from the lists, but was not permitted to re-enter. Combatants, on losing their weapons, were entitled to ask their attendants for a fresh supply. The tournament *en masse* used to be followed by the Joust (*das Stechen im hohen Zeug*, or *Hastiludium*), to which, in some parts of Germany, only those knights were admitted who had already fought in the Behord. The champions, whilst running against each other, endeavoured to hit the breast or the body. Each party sought, by skilful evolutions, to avoid the thrust, or to let the lance glide off. In some of these military games, the shield was not attached to the arm, but to the breast. If such a shield was struck in the centre, it fell to the ground. A game of this description is represented in Plate 45. When the lance was properly aimed, and struck the body, the adversary was unhorsed, and the weapon was dashed to pieces. This shattering of lances was often mutual and simultaneous. If a combatant fell, or if his lance remained uninjured, while that of his adversary was broken, he was considered as vanquished.

German works on tournaments, of the sixteenth and seventeenth centuries, enumerate various military sports, among which the following are more particularly noticed. The *Geschiftrennen*, which was a hastilude with targets or pectoral shields. The *Bundrennen* was performed without body armour. The tourneyers merely bore the pectoral shield, with padding beneath. Gorget and visor, consisting of one piece, were rivetted to the shield, (Plates 60 and 40). At the assault across the barriers, (*Stechen über Schranken*) the combatants were separated from each other by boarded partitions. On approaching each other, they were therefore under the necessity of suddenly stopping their horses. The *Gesellenstechen*, (the hastilude in company) consisted, as the name implies, of a tournament in which the tourneyers attacked each other in groups, until only one victor was left to triumph over the rest. This game differed from the Behord, in so far as it required a smaller number of combatants, and the victor had to try his skill against another victor, until only one remained in the lists as the most gallant champion.

Tournaments of a more serious character (*Jousts à l'outrance*, in German *Scharfstechen*), were fought with sharp weapons. They occurred more rarely, and only between knights who belonged to different nations, or who were subjects of different sovereigns. These fights were occasioned by national or personal animosities.

It is notorious that the tourneying knights received from the ladies some ornamental portion of dress, such as favours, streamers, etc., with which they decorated their helmets, arms, or lances. If such a sign of favour were lost in the heat of the encounter, a new one was granted. These gifts naturally left much scope for the display of courtesy. Not unfrequently, successful knights presented their ladies with the valuable prizes gained during the combat, in return for the encouragement they had received. The forms in which tournaments were proclaimed by the heralds, suggest that the sports were mainly undertaken to do honour and afford diversion to the ladies.

Tournaments were terminated by the command of the judges. An announcement of the termination being made by the *Conclusion of Tournaments.* king-at-arms, the trumpeters gave the signal of retreat. The standard-bearers of the leaders headed the cavalcade, and were followed by other standard-bearers and knights. The latter were allowed to continue their exercises until they reached their temporary residences. The knight of honour rode up to the platform occupied by the ladies On returning from the lists, his helmet was carried before him by the appointed bearer. Every evening, when the sports of the day were over, and also on the two days previous to the tourney, banquets were given at the expense of the two leaders, and under the auspices of the judges. At the concluding banquet, the knight of honour returned the female head-dress, the distinguishing mark of his office, to the lady from whom he had received it, and was entitled to a kiss as his recompense.

At the distribution of the prizes, every blow was taken into careful consideration. He who threw down the horse and its rider, by hitting the saddle, forfeited his claim to the prize. He, also, who struck the leg of his opponent, lost his title to a prize. To unhelm oneself twice, was tantamount to not having broken a lance. The prize was gained by strictly following the rules of the tourney, as well as by giving proofs of dexterity and vigour.

On awarding the prize, a procession was formed by the trumpeters, *Award of Prizes.* the poursuivants of the herald, and three ladies, who were conducted by the judges and the other knights. One lady carried the prize. This lay on some ornamental female dress, the ends of which were held by the other two ladies. The first of the ladies offered the prize to the victorious knight, who knelt before her and had the rightful claim to a kiss. King Réné alludes to three prizes which ordinarily were granted. A golden stick for the knight who had excelled in thrusting his lance; a ruby worth a 1000 dollars to him who had broken the greatest number of lances; and a diamond worth a 1000 dollars to the tourneyer who had fought longest without unhelming himself. The prizes distributed at tournaments, independently of the banquets, proved exceedingly expensive to the two leaders. Hence, the frequent complaints, during the age of chivalry, that the nobles ruined themselves by giving these feasts. The other knights, also, who took part in the tourney, were heavily taxed for their amusements.

They were obliged to give fees, determinable by the judges, to the herald and to the poursuivants. The same officers also received gratuities from the victorious knights. The changes in the nature of property and of pecuniary relations, during the sixteenth century, exercised some influence in causing the discontinuance of the tournament.

In Germany, the last imperial tournament was held in 1487. At the court of France, this knightly sport took place for the last time in 1559, when Henry II. was mortally wounded, by the splinter of a lance entering one of his eyes. In the sixteenth century, when the nobility abandoned heavy armour, as utterly useless in the new system of warfare, the tournament degenerated into simple equestrian display, or ended in senseless mummery.

Nearly all the illustrations of tournaments in the present work are of the fifteenth century. Plates 33, 42, 51, and 60 are *The Illustrations in this Work.* copied from a MS. in the Library of Dresden, and represent the hastiludes of the Dukes John, John Frederic, and Augustus of Saxony. Plates 31 and 32 are copied from a MS. in the Library of Gotha. The latter is given as the effigy of a Margrave of Brandenbourg, but the armour is in the French style, and accords with the rules of King Réné. The fleurs-de-lis on the caparison of the horse, likewise point to French fashion. The next series of illustrations is copied from the Dresden Collection of Engravings, (the *Kupferstich-Cabinet*). The originals are painted on parchment, and contain marginal explanations, which, however, are not always to be relied on. The armour in Plate 35, the date of which cannot extend beyond the end of the fourteenth century, is there asserted to be of the tenth century. Plate 36 is correctly attributed to the age of the Emperor Frederic Barbarossa. Plate 37 is marked with the year 1362; this date may be correct. Although, at that time, mixed armour was in fashion, it is possible that complete plate-armour was already introduced. The commencement of one style of equipment, and the abandonment of another, cannot be minutely determined, from want of the requisite data. The illustrations which follow belong to the fifteenth century. Plate 38 exhibits armour of 1410; 43 is of 1482; 40 represents a *Geschiftrennen*, a kind of Joust which has already been described; 41 is not quite intelligible. In the explanation, it is described by the term of *Pfannenrennen*, literally, a Joust with the Pan, in which the champion wore, under the emblazoned surcoat, a cuirass, and a target in the shape of a gridiron. It is further stated, that this combat was very dangerous, and a bier was carried into the lists behind the duellers. From this allusion, it is to be inferred, that such jousts took place at judicial combats. The red attire of one of the parties supports this conjecture, for in the Assizes of Jerusalem, it is ordained that the combatants, suspected of murder, should appear in red garments. Also the *Sachsenspiegel* lays down the rule, that a coat of this colour should be worn at duels. At the same time, it is to be presumed that the combat with dangerous weapons was not, in all instances, carried to an extreme, that proved fatal to one or other of the contending parties. The copies taken from the above-mentioned *Turnierbuch,* Plates 34, 43, 52, and 53, contain, besides the delineations of the tourneyers, those of the attendants, trumpeters, and drummers. Plate 54 depicts armour of a later period, which is preserved in Dresden. It was worn by the Elector Christian I. The Plates 56 to 59 are copied from the *Fechtbuch,* (book of fighting) of Hector Mairs, of Augsburg, and take their date from the first half of the fifteenth century.

TRIALS BY SINGLE COMBAT.

Legal duels, the most common and most important ordeals of the middle ages, were known to the Germans in the remotest times. A trace of them occurs in a passage of Tacitus, in which he states, that the Germans believed their warriors were favoured by a special presidency of the deity. The same reliance, though not universally predominant, justified, in the middle ages, the retention of duels. During the reign of Charlemagne's successors, the church sought to weaken the belief in the decision of these ordeals. The writings of laymen, and laws enacted by rulers of a later age, had a similar tendency of counteracting the effect of these superstitious trials, and of referring the issue of a duel to a superiority of skill and physical force, rather than to a miraculous intervention of providence. The proceedings at these ordeals are minutely described in the Capitularies of Charlemagne, and in subsequent codes of law. Justice being then chiefly regulated by precedents, the decision by wager of battle was, undoubtedly, of frequent occurrence. The best information for our purpose is to be derived from the description given in the Assizes of Jerusalem.

Trials by Duel.

Duels were fought for the pupose of settling the rights of property, or for avenging the commission of crime. In cases of disputes relative to property, it was necessary that the objects of contention should be worth more than one mark of silver. It is to be inferred from various passages in the Assizes of Jerusalem, that such combats were chiefly designed for the adjustment of disputed territorial claims. Considering the ancient value of landed property, disputes could only arise about extensive pieces of land. Duels could also be demanded in some special cases, as for example, in reference to horse-dealing, denial of a debt, refusal of paying wages, security for a debtor, loans, sales of leprous slaves, and other suits that bore upon the loss of property, and involved the accusation of fraud.

Purpose of Ordeals.

Crimes were tried by duels, if they included such acts as murder, manslaughter, rape, infliction of a wound, neglect in the discharge of feudal service, treason, and deprivation of, or exclusion from a rightful possession. Witnesses at court, whose veracity was impugned, could be challenged to fight a duel; in which case, the challenger, after they had been sworn, took hold of their hands, and gave their gloves to the presiding judge. Even jurors at the Assizes, who were suspected of partiality, could be challenged, if they chose to accept the summons. If the court was unanimous in its decision, the challenger had to fight on one and the same day, with all the judges of the court.

As a general principle, a knight was not bound to fight with a man of the civic class, or with a nobleman who had not received the accolade. If a commoner felt aggrieved on account of bodily injuries he had sustained at the hands of a knight, and a duel was to serve as evidence, the injured man had to appoint a knight to represent his cause. This law held good even in cases of murder. If, however, a knight summoned a plebeian witness to fight a duel, he was obliged to appear with arms peculiar to the inferior orders. According to the Laws of St. Louis, a knight, who

Knights and Plebeians.

was challenged by a commoner for grave offences, was required to fight on horseback.

If a knight challenged a commoner, the duel took place on foot. Ladies, men above the age of sixty, and persons bodily disabled from fighting, could appoint a champion. Such representatives often served for hire, or expected a considerable emolument for their exertions; their occupation was, therefore, held as one of a degrading nature.

If the challenge had been legally approved, both parties were Preparations for the Trial. required to offer their gloves to the feudal lord or his judicial representative. The contending parties were then taken into custody, but were better treated than common prisoners. After an exchange of the gaged gloves, the parties were no longer at liberty to settle their disputes without the consent of the feudal superior, and according to the Assizes of Jerusalem, the three parties were then required to be unanimous. According to English law, the sovereign had authority to settle disputes and forbid duels. After the delivery of the gloves to the presiding lord, a respite of some days was given before the combat took place. Three days were allowed in cases of murder or manslaughter, and forty days for other offences. When that time had expired, the parties were led to the place of battle. The equipment was, in some instances, subject to certain restrictions. According to the Assizes of Jerusalem, a knight, accused of murder or homicide, appeared on foot, without helmet and hauberk. His dress consisted of a red coat, which reached to the knees, and the sleeves were cut off to reach the elbows. He also wore red breeches and stockings, but no shoes. His only defensive armour was a shield, which covered the whole body, and even projected one hand's breadth above his head. The shield contained two small holes, through which the combatant could watch his antagonist. He carried also a lance and two swords, one attached to the belt, the other to the shield. In other instances, the knight was fully equipped with his chivalric suit, being provided with hauberk, breeches, a padded under-garment, which covered the lower part of his body, a shield, a visored helmet, a lance, and two swords. The helmet was furnished with a sharp rim, and the surface of the shield displayed two spikes. The rim of the shield could be armed with any number of spikes.

One sword was fastened to the belt, and the other hung on the saddle. The lists were surrounded by trenches and palings. Until the moment of the conflict, the hostile parties were strictly guarded and kept in separate cells. Their weapons were carefully examined, and compared with each other, lest a combatant might have an advantage over the other. The champions being armed, they were led into the lists. The superintendents of the lists administered to the contending parties an oath upon the Gospel, each of them being required to affirm that neither his person nor his horse was secretly guarded, and above all, that he had employed no witchcraft. The defendant was then desired to kneel down, and swear that he was innocent. The accuser had to seize him by the hand, to call him a perjured man, and to repeat his former accusation, by another oath. The superintendents of the combat then separated the two champions, and on each side of the lists, a caution was proclaimed, that no man should, in any language, utter anything that might tend to benefit or afford a hint to one or the other of the combatants. Persons acting in defiance of this warning, forfeited life and property to their lord. In the regulations of duels by Philip the Fair, even the act of spitting is forbidden.

In duels relating to murder, the body of the slain was carried into the lists and uncovered. An accuser, represented Trial for Murder. by a champion, had his seat behind the lists, where he was vigilantly guarded, lest he should give a hint to the champion. The latter was sworn in a manner similar to that we have just described.

The champions then put on their helmets, mounted their horses, and took up their shields and lances. The attendants led them apart by the bridle, and assigned to them the positions they should occupy in the lists. The presiding lord then gave the order, " Let them meet each other," and the encounter commenced. Commoners wore, on such occasions, red blouses or coats, and gartered stockings, without shoes. Their heads were shorn. Their weapons consisted of large shields, and clubs which were made of taurine sinews, with a thick knob at the top, and a bone point at the lower end. This species of arms was generally used by hired champions, and of great antiquity at legal duels. The club and the shield are mentioned in the Capitularies as the weapons of the ordeal in question. The appointed superintendents remained at a distance so long as the combat lasted, but as soon as one of the duellists was defeated, they drew near to watch every word that was uttered. If a confession of guilt was made, the duel terminated, the parties were separated, and the vanquished individual was handed over to the presiding lord. The final proceedings were in harmony with the cruelty of the whole trial. According to the Assizes of Jerusalem, the convicted criminals were dragged from the lists, and put to death by means of the rope. If the delinquent had availed himself of the aid of a champion, and had produced a witness, all the three were hanged. If a woman was involved in such an ordeal, she was burnt. In the Regulations of Philip the Fair, it is enjoined that the armour should be torn from the body of the vanquished, and be scattered in the lists.

In trials for encroachments on property, the Assizes of Jerusalem Trials relative to Property. required the execution of the vanquished champion, while his inculpated employer only lost his law suit, and as a citizen, forfeited his honour.* This rule, however, was not of general validity. A law of Louis the Debonair ordained that a duellist, guilty of perjury, should lose his right hand, a punishment which was prescribed in many codes of law. Du Cange cites an ancient statute,

* That is to say, his testimony, as a witness, lost its validity in the eyes of the law.

which gave to territorial lords the option of ordering the execution or the mutilation of the unsuccessful duellist. Minor trespasses appear to have been visited by mutilating the unfortunate convict. If a knight struck a citizen, and his guilt was proven in a duel with a knightly representative of the citizen, the offender lost his right hand. These duels having been customary in the early settlements of the German tribes, retained, in all parts, some of their characteristics, though with modifications. In the *Sachsenspiegel*, for example, the duel is carried on in gloves, and the number of duelling swords is left to the option of the champions. During the later part of the middle ages, the knights of Germany and other countries fought in full armour. Plate 61 appears to represent such a duel, in which the champions are unhorsed, and have abandoned their weapons. Their shields are bordered with spikes, as ordained in the Assizes of Jerusalem. Plate 43 has already been noticed as probably representing a legal duel. Such combats were held, even in the fifteenth and sixteenth centuries, although the belief in their power of eliciting the truth had been shaken even in the thirteenth century. In France, the last ordeals by combat took place under Francis I. in the years 1538 and 1547. Among the Germans and the English, trials of this description ceased before the sixteenth century.

THE END.

REFERENCES TO THE AUTHORITIES

CONSULTED IN THE PRESENT WORK.

PAGE	LINE		
1	7	They are mentioned	Tacitus, Germania, c. 7.
1	26	What was the	Ibid.
2	2	Thus the Cherusci	Tacitus, Ann., 11. [p. 272.
2	10	In Iceland	Grimm, Rechtsalterthümer,
2	19	The nobles were	Am. Marcellinus, xvii., 12.
3	15	Noble Courtiers	Grimm, p. 250.
3	22	The Salic Law	Grimm, 272.
3	28	The Visigothic	Sid. Apollodorus, Epist.
3	33	The advantages	Germania, 13.
4	14	According to	Jornandes, c. 5. [p. 325.
4	15	They also wore	Aschbach's Westgothen,
4	20	The mass	Grimm, p. 283—300.
6	10	These dignitaries	Marculfi, Form. 12 and 14.
7	12	The Frankish	Savigny, Zur Rechtsgeschichte des Adels, p.17. (In the Transactions of the Academy of Berlin, 1836).
7	19	The Salic Law	Grimm, p. 272.
8	19	Laws enacted	Schmidt, Geschichte der Deutschen, Vol. II.
8	28	At the same time	Grimm, 298.
8	34	To escape the	Capitularia, A.D. 805.
11	4	Besides the practice	Grimm, 326—331.
12	23	Even Tacitus	Germania, xxiv.
13	9	Thus for example	Gibbon, Vol. V., c. 14.
13	17	The horseman	Ibid., Vol. II., c. xiv. and Vegetius, de Re Milit. Lib. I. c. 20.
13	23	The Franks	Gibbon, Vol. VI. c. 38.
15	29	The names assumed	Mabillon, Traité Diplomatique, I. c. 7, and Nouveau Traité, II., p. 563.
16	3	The introduction of	Mémoires de l'Académie des Inscriptions, T. XX, p. 579.
16	21	In the reigns of	Carpentier, Gloss. v. nobilitare.
17	2	In France	Du Cange, Dissert. sur Joinville, 10.
18	23	In England	Hallam's Middle Ages, II. c. 8.
20	14	We now proceed	Ensayo historico-critico sobre la antiqua legislacion y principales cuerpos de los reynos de Leon y Castilla, por Marina.
23	20	The Aborigines of	Bernal Diaz del Castilla, Conquista de la Nueva España, L. XII. c. 13.
23	33	The luckless freemen	Bianca Comment. in Schotti Hispania illustrata, T. II.
24	2	It extended	Ranke's Fürsten und Völker von Süd-Europa, T. I., p. 249.
25	4	The nobles	Muratori Dissert. 49.
29	36	In England	Hallam's Middle Ages, II., c. 9.
30	20	Boucicault, for	Bouchet, Hist. de Louis de la Trémouille, p. 57.
30	28	The boy	Grimm, p. 411.
31	7	In reference	Hist. de Boucicault, ed. Godefroy.
31	36	Early acquaintance	La Palaye, pp. 19 and 20.
32	27	It is related	Brantôme, Cap. Fr.I. p.12.
33	1	Respecting outward	La Palaye, I. pp. 287 & 333 and Du Cange, v. Calcaria aurea et argentea.
33	24	Joinville	Hist. de St. Louis, pp. 20 and 21.
33	28	Froissart	Chronique et Histoire, T. III., p. 31.
34	1	When a young	Grimm, p. 416.
36	1	On some occasions	Duran, Romancero, Madr. 1832, Parte II. p. 63.
36	10	The newly installed	La Palaye, I. 74.
36	20	It is related	Froissart, T. III.
37	34	We find notices	Tacitus, Germ., c. xiii.
37	36	Charlemagne	Du Cange, v. arma dare.
38	26	The latter	La Palaye, p. 352.
39	2	The bannerets	Ibid., T. I., p. 304.
39	25	A strange specimen	Ibid., II., p 13.
40	9	Ladies being present	Roman du Perceforest, XX., Table III.
40	27	At another time	Froissart, I., pp. 43 & 44, (ed. Menard).
40	37	At the siege	Froissart, II., p. 20.
41	9	Even legislation	De Marca, Marca Hispanica, p. 1428.
41	22	Prisoners were	La Palaye, I., p. 309.
41	24	After the battle	Froissart, I., c. xvi.
42	17	An Italian	Muratori, Script.Re.Italic. VIII., p. 351.
42	32	Bert. Du Guesclin	Hist. de B. Du Guesclin, p. 303.
43	7	The following story	Joinville, p. 43.
43	23	In the romances	Duran, Romancero, II., pp. 83 and 113.
44	1	Chivalry extended	Du Cange, v. Arma and Sanguis, and La Palaye, I., 227.
44	19	His shield	La Palaye, I., p. 316 and Du Cange, v. arma reversata.
44	31	In some parts	Grimm, p. 712.
44	34	For minor offences	Du Cange, v. mensale dividere.
45	9	Du Guesclin	Histoire, &c. p. 410.
45	11	In the first	Froissart, I., p. 33.
45	17	Such a vow	Olivier de la Marche, Mémoires, p. 412 et seq. and Grimm, p. 901.
46	5	In the ancient	Grimm, p. 251.
46	31	In the Assizes	Assises de la Baisse Cour, § 47.
47	5	At the wedding	Sid. Apollinaris, Epistolarum Libri, IV., 20.
48	7	The defeat	Meyrick, William I.
48	10	Though the German	Du Cange, v. sagittare.
48	22	In cases of hostile	Grimm, p. 162.
49	1	Vegetius	De Re Militari, IV., 22.
49	18	The Roman See	Du Cange, v. Ballistarii.
49	36	Such a corps	Meyrick, Henry VI., Edward IV., Henry ·VII. and Henry VIII.
50	7	At Poitiers	Froissart, I., 162.
50	12	An ordonnance	Meyrick, Edward III. and Edward IV.
50	28	In Arragon	Ibid., Henry VI.
50	36	When Cortez	Bernal Diaz del Castillo, Hist. de la desc. y conq. de la Nueva España, L. VI., c. 11.
51	9	At first	Du Cange, v. arcubalista.
53	9	Under Henry V,	Meyrick, II., p. 113.
54	33	In a symbolical	Grimm, p. 126.
55	4	In the fifth	Paul Warnefried, Hist. Longob. V., c. 8, and Du Cange, v. mango, petraria, and trabucum.

REFERENCES TO THE AUTHORITIES.

PAGE	LINE		
55	8	*Attila took Aquileia*	Jornandes, c. 42.
55	10	*In* 711	Gibbon, Vol X., c. 51.
55	21	*The Turks made*	Ibid., Vol. XII., c. 67.
55	24	*The Spaniards*	Bernal Diaz del Castillo, Nueva España, I., 8, c. 11.
55	30	*The wooden towers*	Gulielmus Tyr., IV., 15.
56	27	*The Petraries*	Ibid., III., 5.
56	38	*During the third*	Meyrick, I., p. 75.
57	13	*The Greek fire*	Du Cange sur Joinville, pp. 71 and 72; Gloss. v. Ignis Græcus; Gibbon, IX., c. 32.
57	31	*Joinville*	P. 39.
58	17	*Anderne*	Meyrick, II. p. 39.
59	20	*Vegetius*	De Re Militari, IV., p. 17.
59	28	*Meyrick*	I., p. 207.
60	29	*Du Cange*	Gloss., v. catus.
62	14	*William the*	Du Cange, v. arma.
62	22	*Meyrick*	Henry VII.
63	6	*The romance*	Meyrick, I., p. 34.
63	9	*The spear*	Grimm, p. 163 et seq.
63	31	*It formed part*	William of Malmesbury, II., c. vi.
64	34	*The Italian*	Du Cange, v. Sponto.
65	9	*In England*	Meyrick, Henry VIII.
65	22	*Javelins*	Du Cange, v. Javeloces.
65	26	*The Venetians*	Gibbon, X., c. 56.
66	10	*Vegetius*	II., p. 15 and III. p. 14.
66	11	*According to Du Cange*	Gloss., v. Spata.
66	12	*Ordericus Vitalis*	De Persec. Vandal, I.
66	14	*Meyrick*	Introd., p. 64.
66	30	*Meyrick*	II., p. 53.
67	6	*Montfaucon*	Monarchie Française, I., Plate 24.
67	10	*Meyrick*	Vol. II., p. 117.
67	18	*During the later*	Du Cange, v. falcastrum.
67	27	*Meyrick*	II., p. 155.
67	33	*A description*	Meyrick, I., p. 198.
68	36	*Du Cange*	Gloss., v. spatha.
69	3	*A contemporary*	Guil Appulus, T. II., p. 270.
69	16	*Eginhard*	Vita Caroli M., c. 23.
69	23	*An inventory*	Du Cange, v. armatura.
70	11	*The symbolical*	Grimm, pp. 105, 166—169.
70	22	*According to*	Amm. Marcellinus, XVII. p. 107.
70	23	*The Pagan Saxons*	Fredegar, c. 74.
71	1	*The sword*	Grimm, p. 332.
71	10	*This mode*	Carpentier, v. gladius.
71	13	*Among the Goths*	Cassiodorus var. Lib. IV.2.
72	10	*If she selected*	Leges Rip. 58, 18.
72	12	*According to*	Greg. Tur., 14, 18.
72	16	*In the fifteenth*	Grimm, p. 108.
72	34	*Like Hugh Capet*	Du Cange, v. Caliburne.
73	1	*Thus the Cid*	Duran, Romancero, VI., p. 30.
73	13	*This name*	Du Cange, v. saxa.
74	6	*Until a recent*	Grimm, pp. 287, 170, 171.
74	24	*Grimm has shown*	Grimm, p. 64.
75	14	*In England*	Meyrick, II., p. 249.
75	16	*Among the*	Grimm, pp. 64 and 162.
75	29	*Sidonius Apollinaris*	Carm., V.
77	15	*According to*	Meyrick, I., p. 19.
78	8	*Equally uncertain*	Du Cange, v. bombardella.
78	13	*Aeneas Sylvius*	Comment., IV., p. 101.
78	16	*The Florentines*	Muratori Dissert., 26, p. 457.
78	18	*In* 1449	Sismondi, Hist. de l'Italie, IX., p. 341.
78	22	*The French*	Guicciardini, Hist., c. Lib. I., c. 15.
79	1	*Muschet*	Du Cange, v. Muschetta.
79	3	*A balista*	Sanutus Gesta Dei per Francos, pars 3, c. 45.
80	6	*Tacitus*	Germ., VI.
81	22	*In the Assizes*	Haute Cour, § 103.
81	31	*Meyrick*	Henry VI.
82	3	*King Philip*	Ibid., I., 145.
82	31	*Montfaucon*	Monum. Franç. Pl. 215.
83	1	*Owing to such*	Meyrick, I., t. Stephen.
83	24	*The principal*	Amm. Marcell. Lib. 25.
84	1	*Vegetius*	III., 23.
84	25	*Harnisch*	Dietz. Gram. d. roman. Sprachen, I., p. 79.
84	30	*It is said*	Du Cange, v. halsberga.
84	37	*The portrait*	Montfaucon, Mon. Fr. I., Pl. 32.
86	21	*A chronicler*	Meyrick, Richard I.
90	1	*The gloves were*	Grimm, 152—155.
91	31	*Even Tacitus*	Germania, VI.
92	11	*This solemnity*	Grimm, p. 234.
92	14	*Paulus Diaconus*	III., p. 35.
92	15	*Among the Goths*	Cassiodorus, var. 10, 31.
92	17	*With respect*	Gregory of Tours, II., 40, IV., 51, VII., 10.
92	24	*Once more*	Villehardouin, N. 136.
92	34	*Ancient spurs*	Du Cange, calcaria aurea.
93	10	*Saddles are first*	Sid. Apoll., Epist. III., 3.
94	1	*Those martial*	Gibbon, c. X., 58.
94	5	*Tacitus*	Germ., 24.
94	7	*Also Nithard*	III., p. 27.
95	8	*Another German*	Du Cange, v. bohordium.
95	32	*In vain*	Du Cange, v. torn., and Dissert. 6 sur Joinville.
96	2	*The Crusaders*	Gibbon, X. c. 60.
96	30	*The herald*	Les Tournois du Roi Réné, p. 3.
97	10	*Instead of the*	Ibid., p. 8.
97	35	*The helmet*	Ibid., p. 9.
99	10	*Noblemen, guilty*	Ibid., p. 13.
99	28	*If a nobleman*	Ibid., pp. 14, 15.
100	4	*In England*	Meyrick, II., p. 110.
101	28	*Anyone was*	Ibid., p. 181.
101	31	*The tournament*	Du Cange, v. Justa.
102	24	*Tournaments of a*	Ibid. v. torneam. aculeatum Quasi hostile; Dissert. 7 sur Joinville.
102	29	*It is notorious*	Hist. du Chev. Bayard, ed. Godefroy, p. 63.
103	5	*The latter were*	Les Tournois du Roi Réné, p. 23.
105	21	*A trace of them*	Tacitus, Germ., VII.
105	25	*During the reign*	Grimm, p. 929.
106	7	*In cases of*	Assises de Jerus., Baisse Cour, § 138; Haute Cour, § 81.
106	21	*Witnesses at court*	Ibid., Haute Cour, § 74.
106	26	*If the court*	Ibid., § 110.
106	29	*As a general*	Ibid., § 75.
106	31	*If a commoner*	Assises de Jerus., ed. Kausler, I., p. 386.
106	34	*This law*	Ibid., p. 367.
107	3	*If a knight*	Du Cange, v. duellum.
107	4	*Ladies, men*	Ibid., v. campio.
107	9	*If the challenge*	Haute Cour, § 189.
107	12	*After an exchange*	Haute Cour, § 95.
107	23	*According to the*	Ibid., § 102.
107	32	*In other instances*	Ibid., § 301.
108	19	*In the regulations*	Du Cange, v. duellum.
108	31	*Commoners wore*	Haute Cour, § 108.
108	37	*The club and*	Du Cange, campionum arma.
109	15	*In trials for*	Haute Cour, § 104.
109	21	*Du Cange*	Campionis poena.
110	3	*If a knight*	Assises de Jerusalem, ed. Kausler, I., p. 386.
110	8	*In the*	Sachsenspiegel, I., § 13.

INDEX.

CORRIGENDA.

Page 3, line 16, read *Courtiers, according to Grimm.*
Page 21, line 31, read *from " Hijo d'Algo."*
Page 66, line 11, read *According to Du Cange, it was known.*
Page 91, line 26, read *Plate 26, Fig. 4, represents the Pavise.*

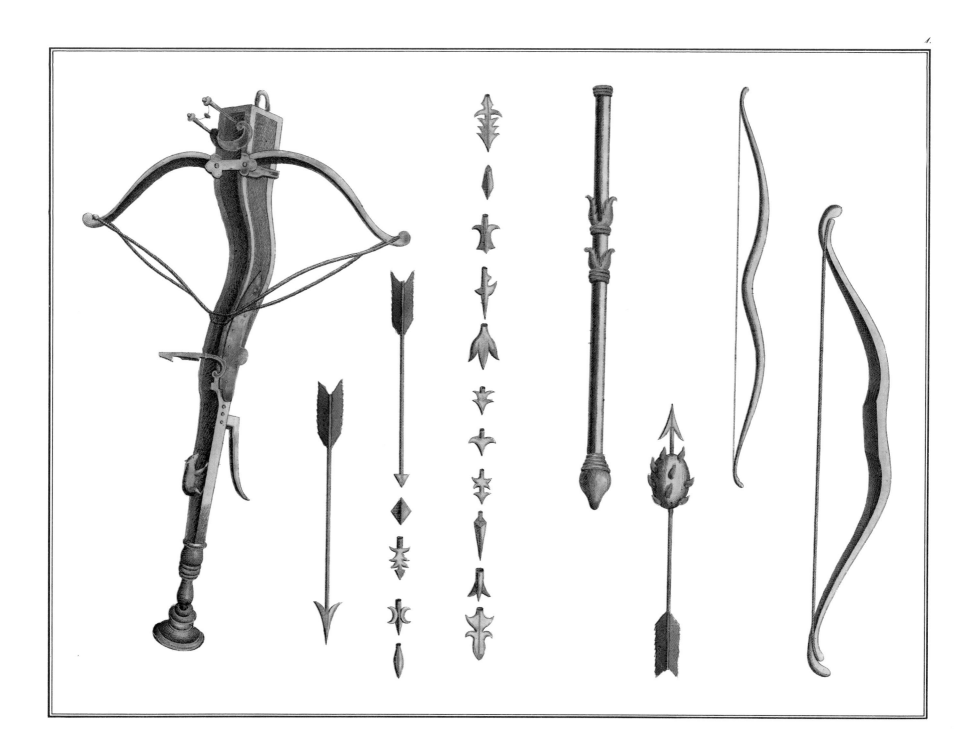

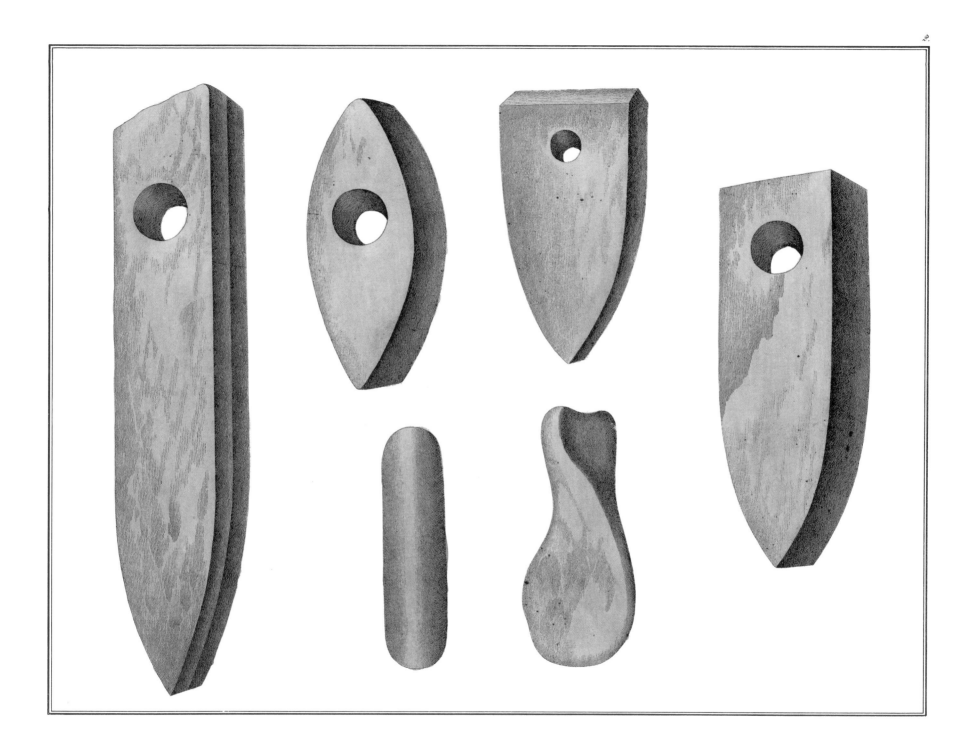

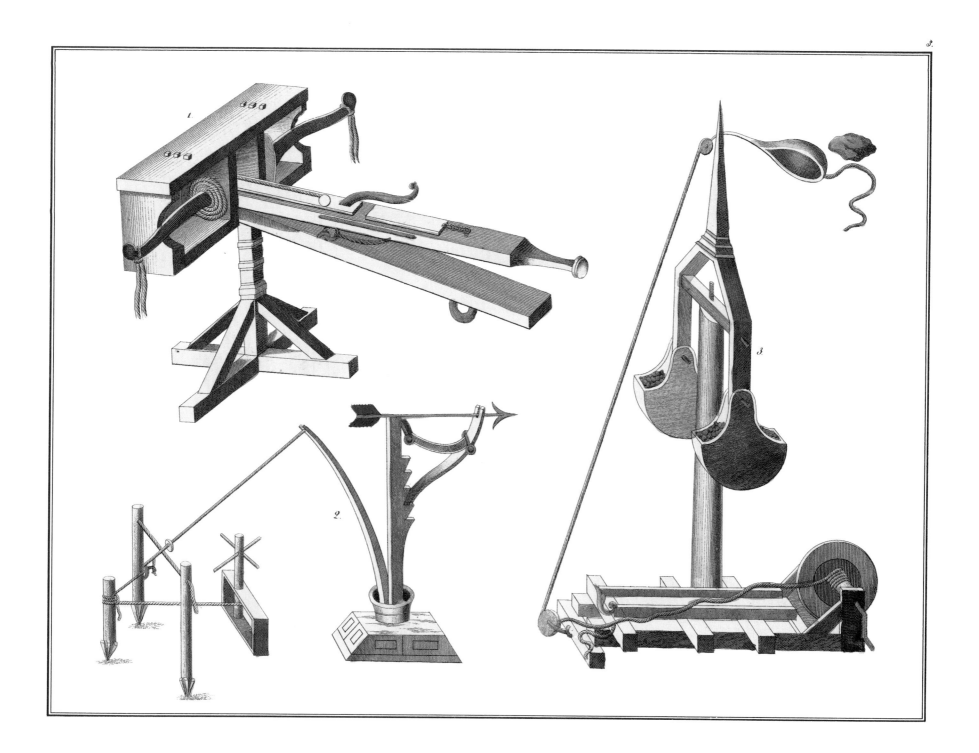

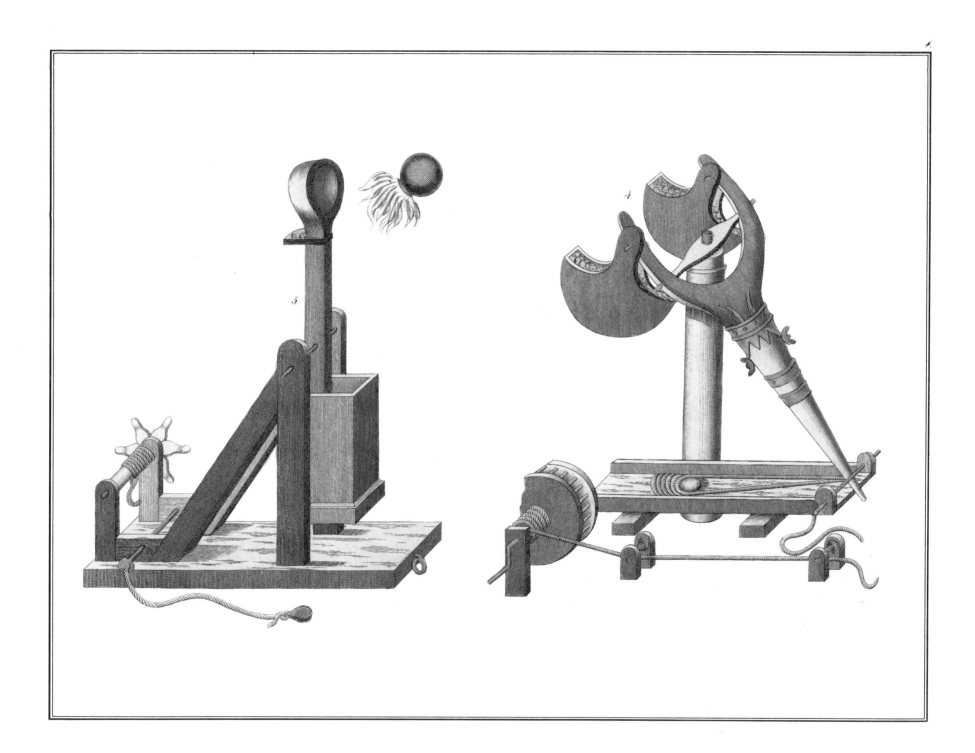

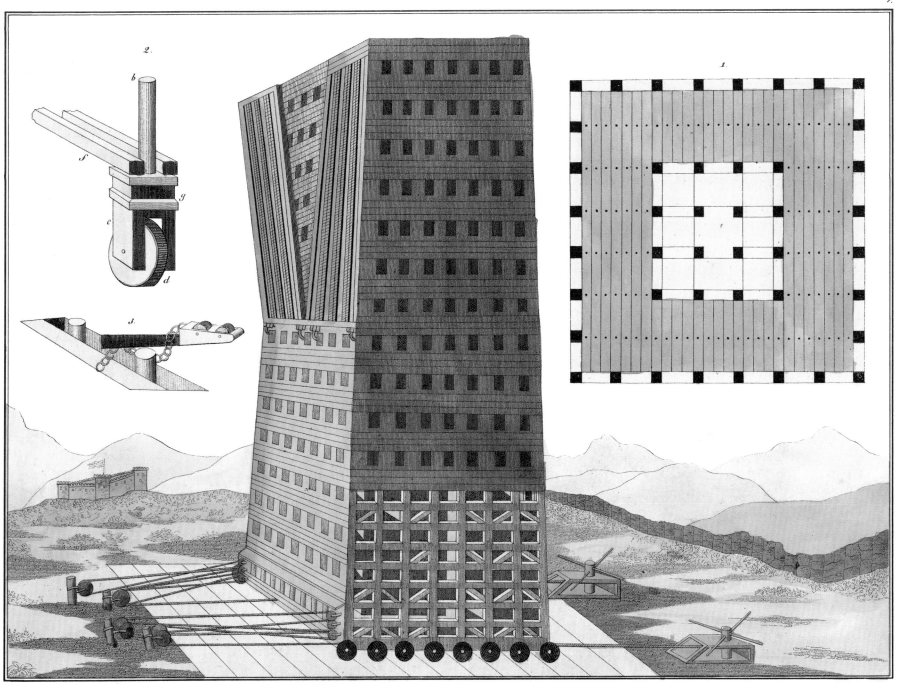

7.

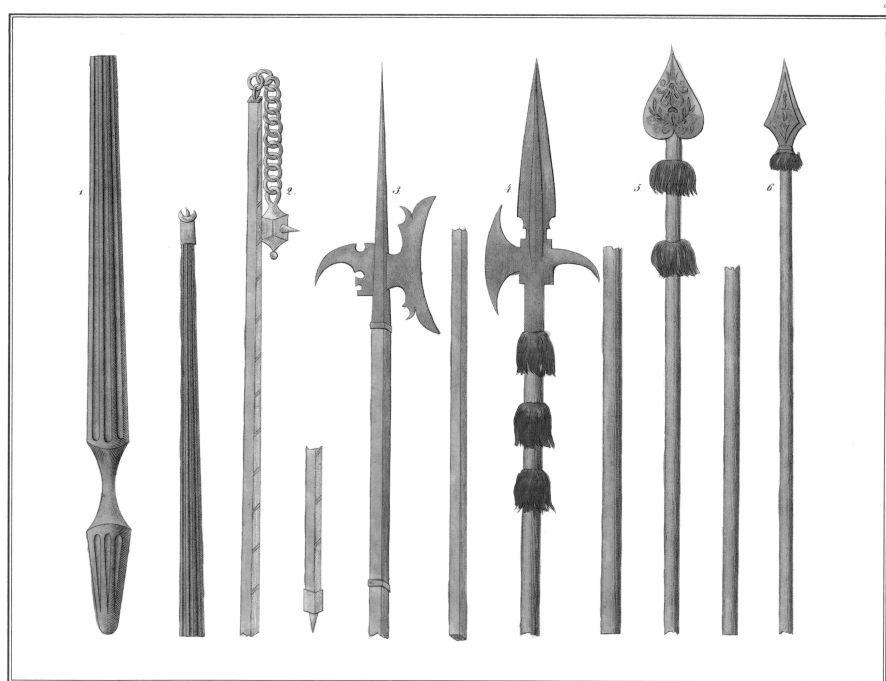

1. 2. 3. 4. 5. 6.

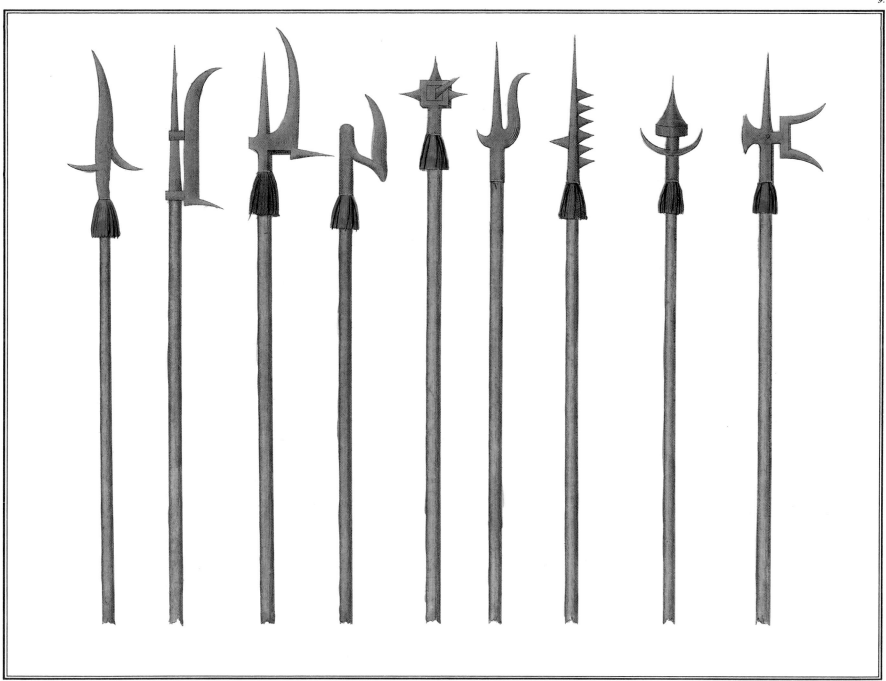

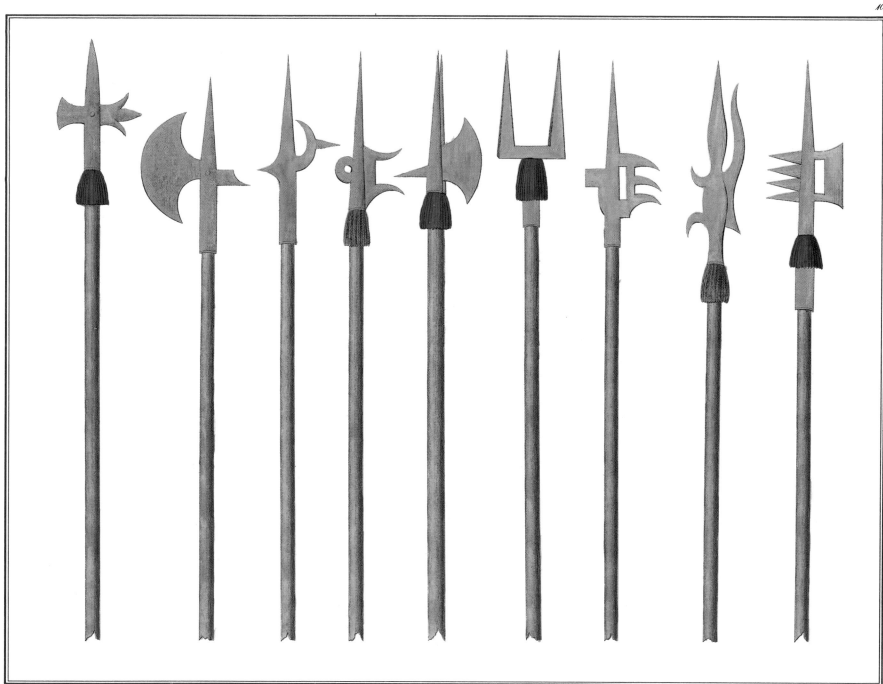

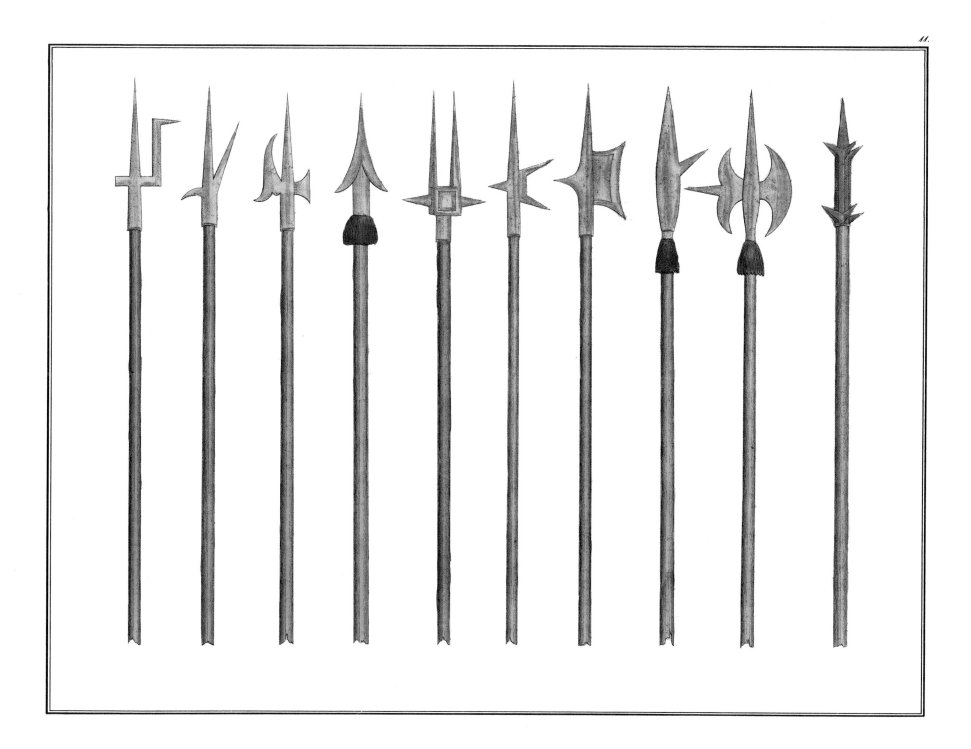

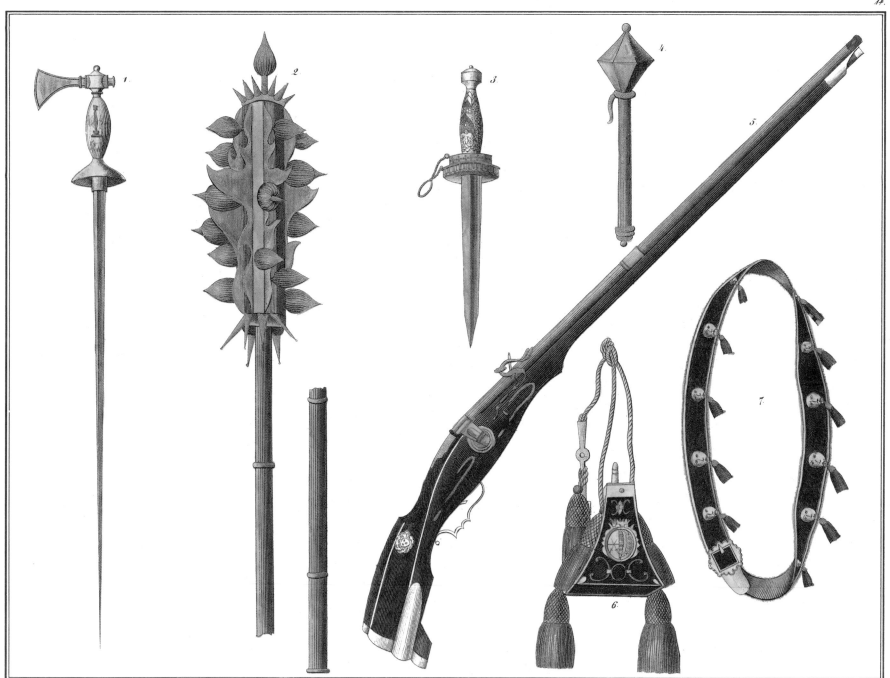

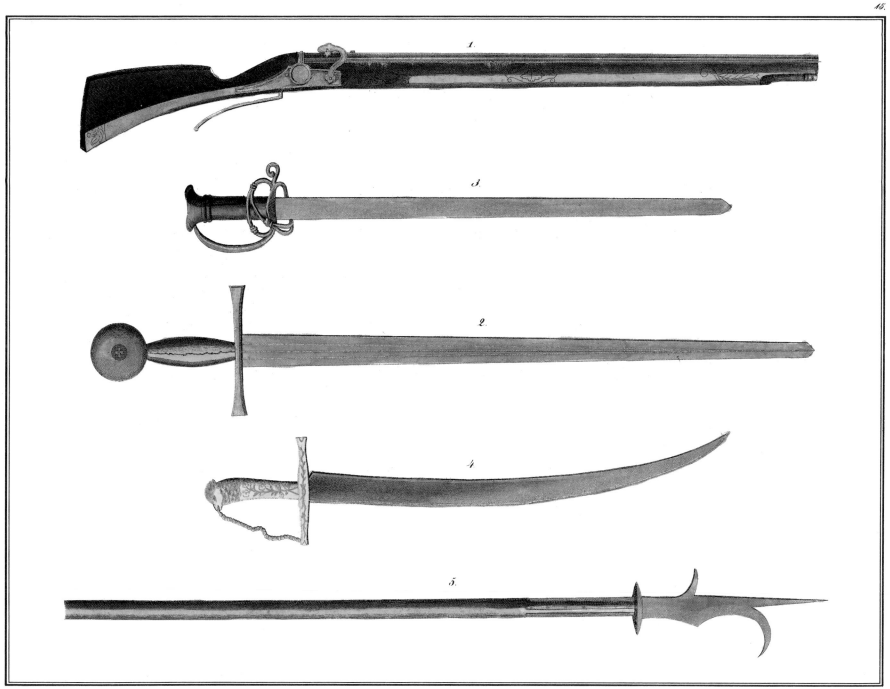

1.

3.

2.

4.

5.

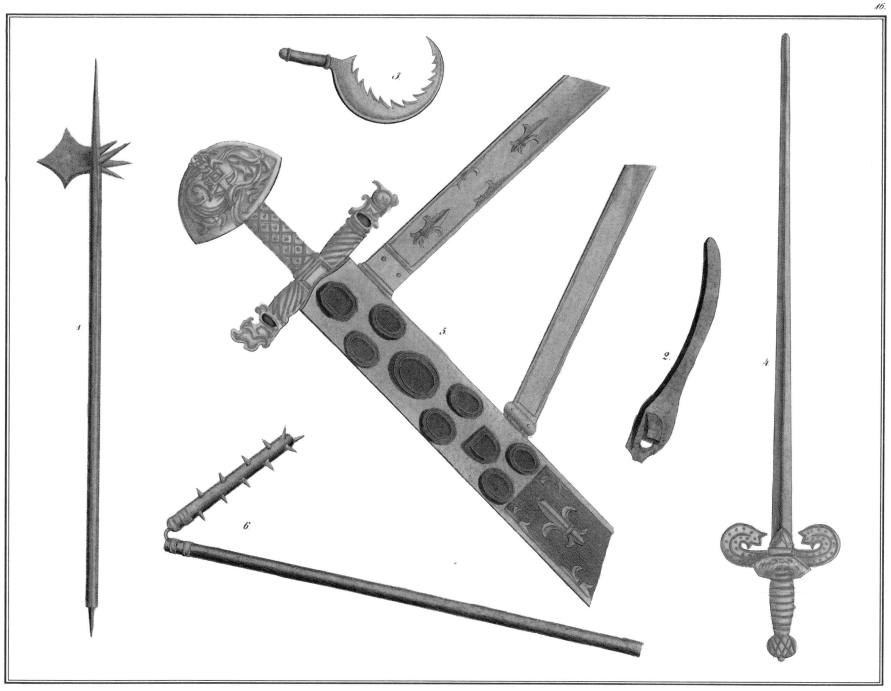

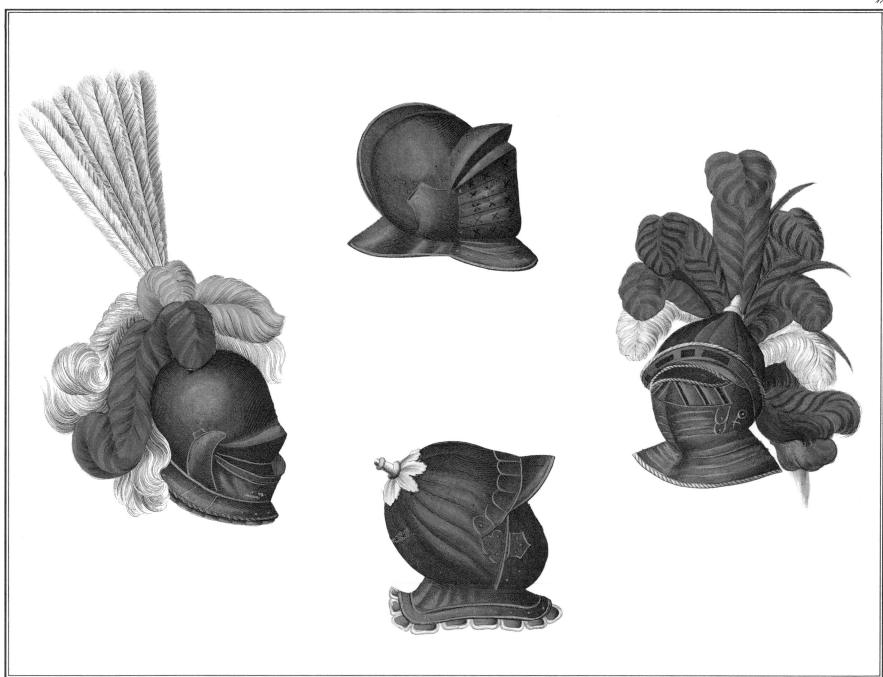

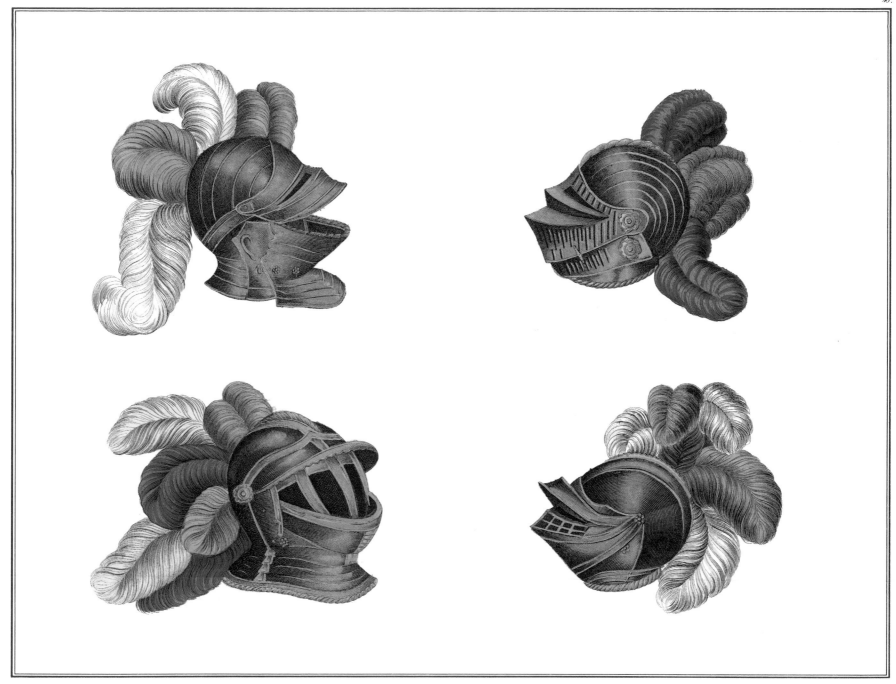

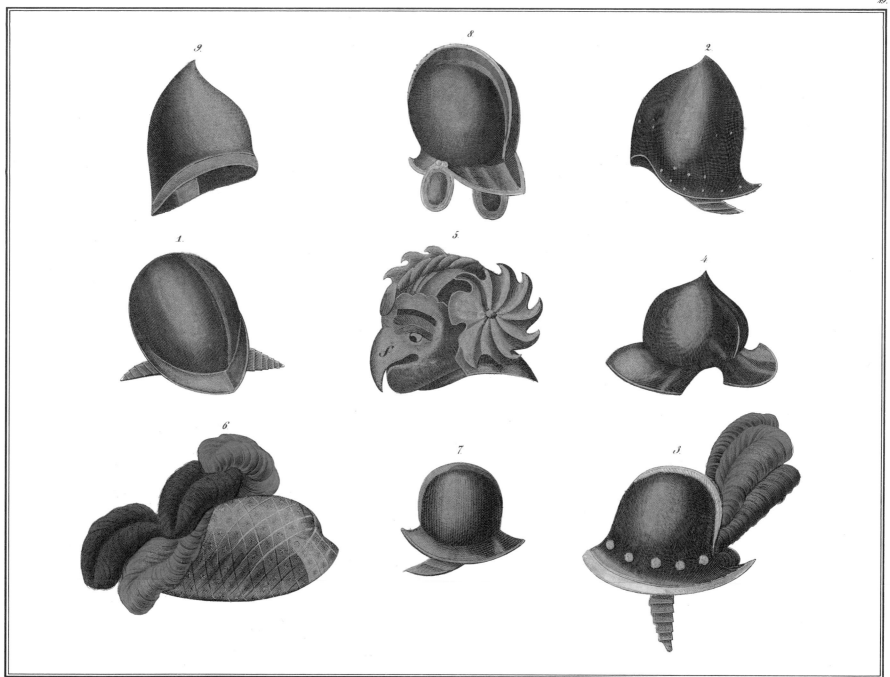

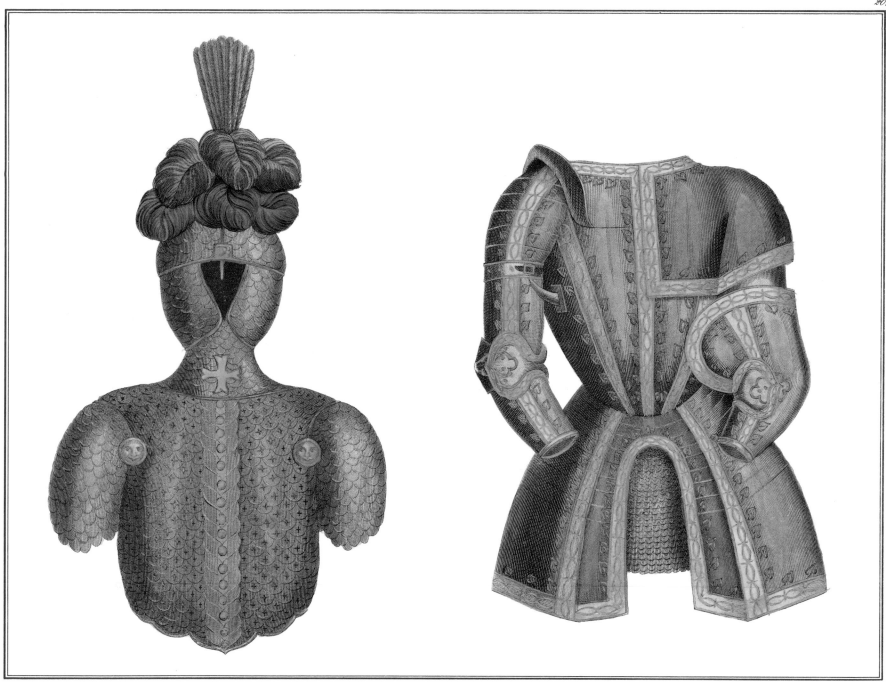

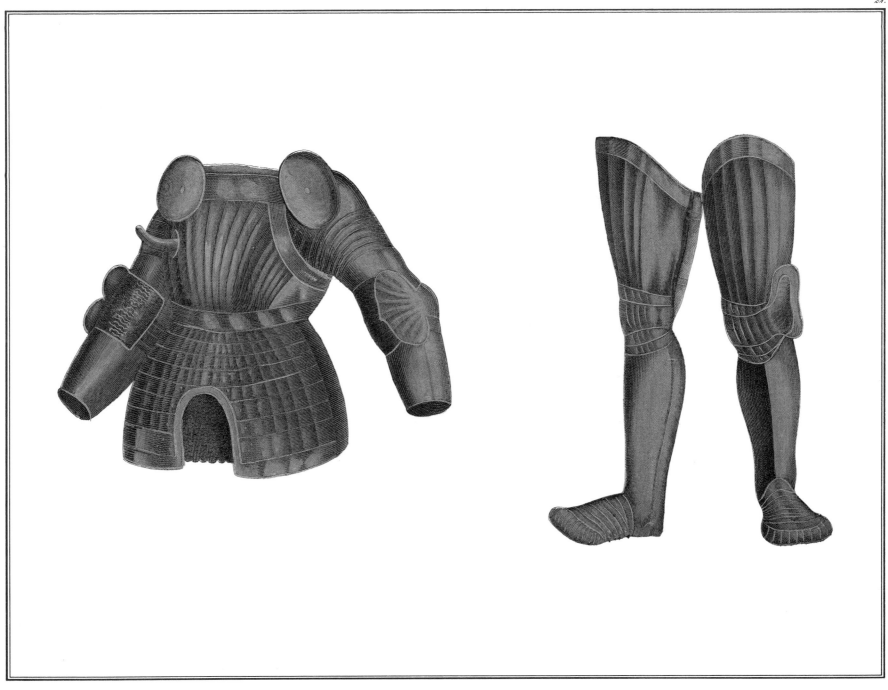

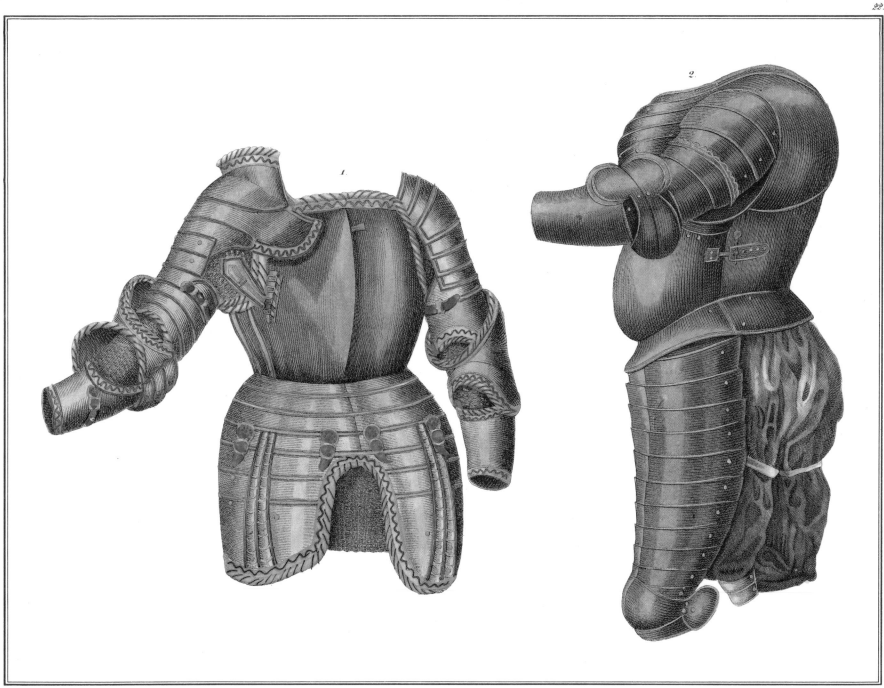

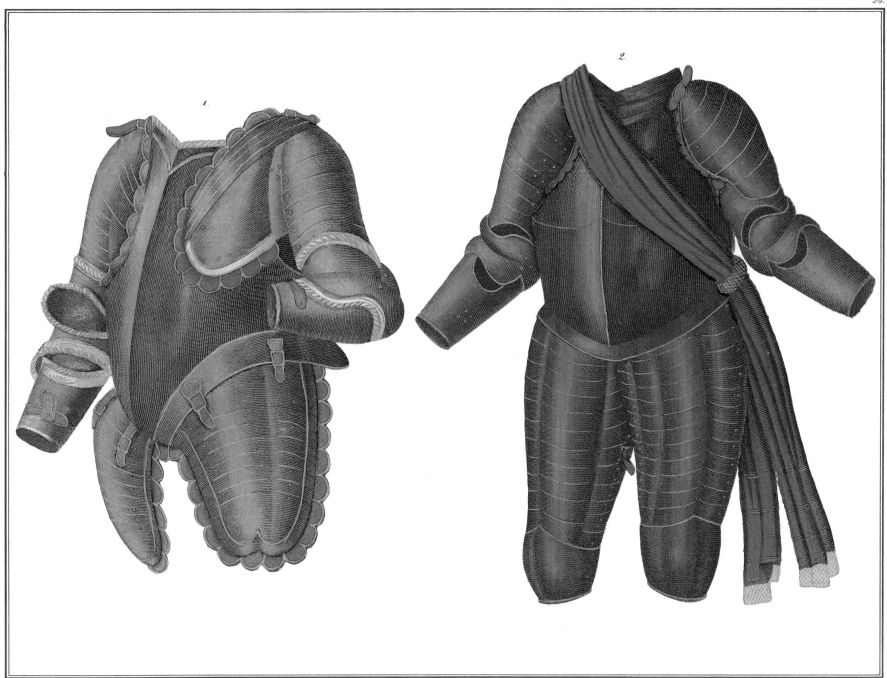

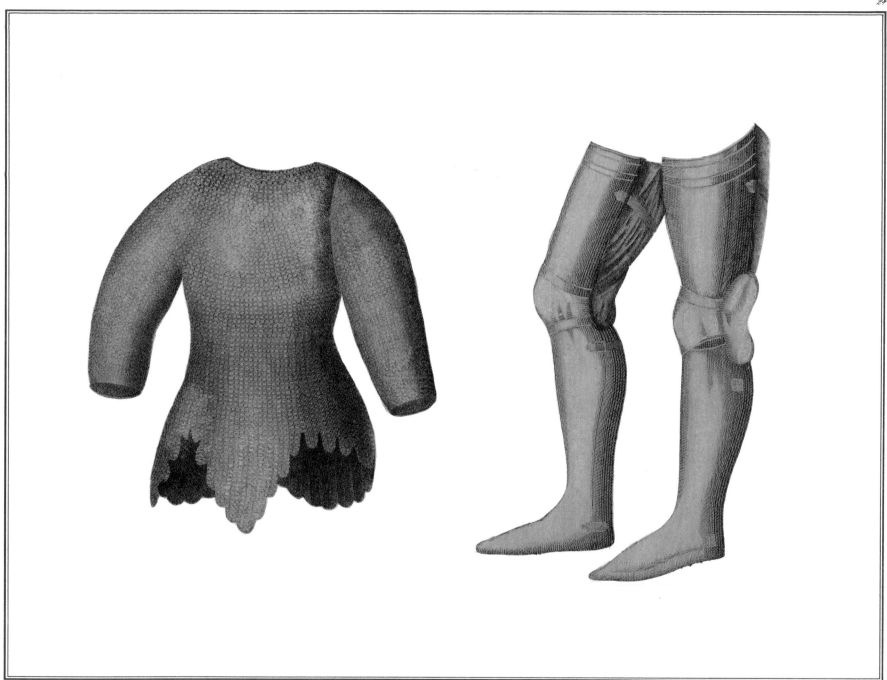

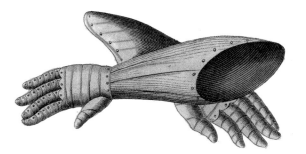

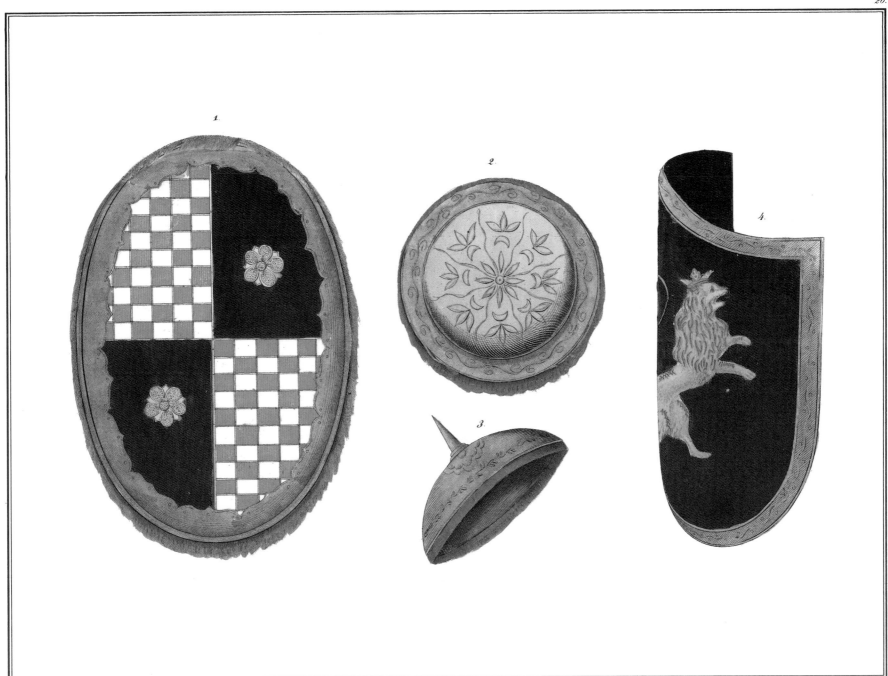

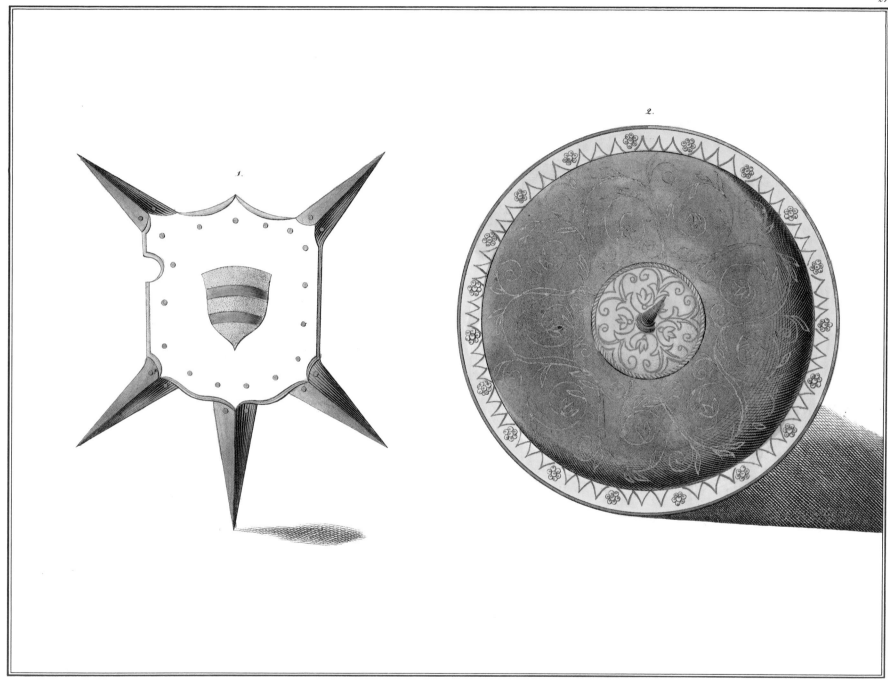

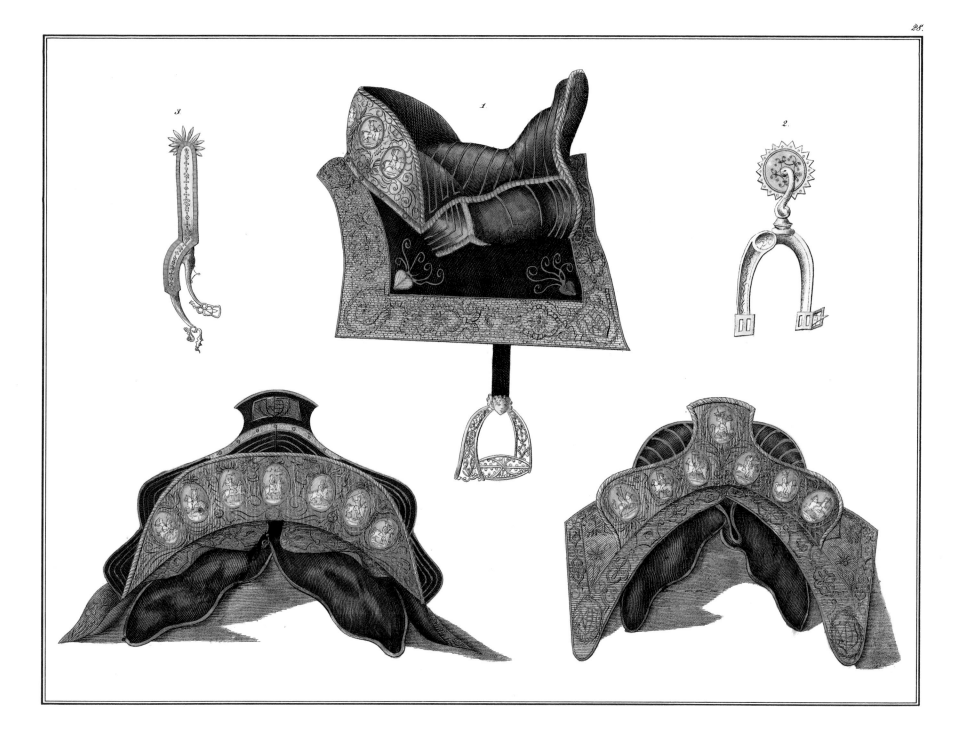

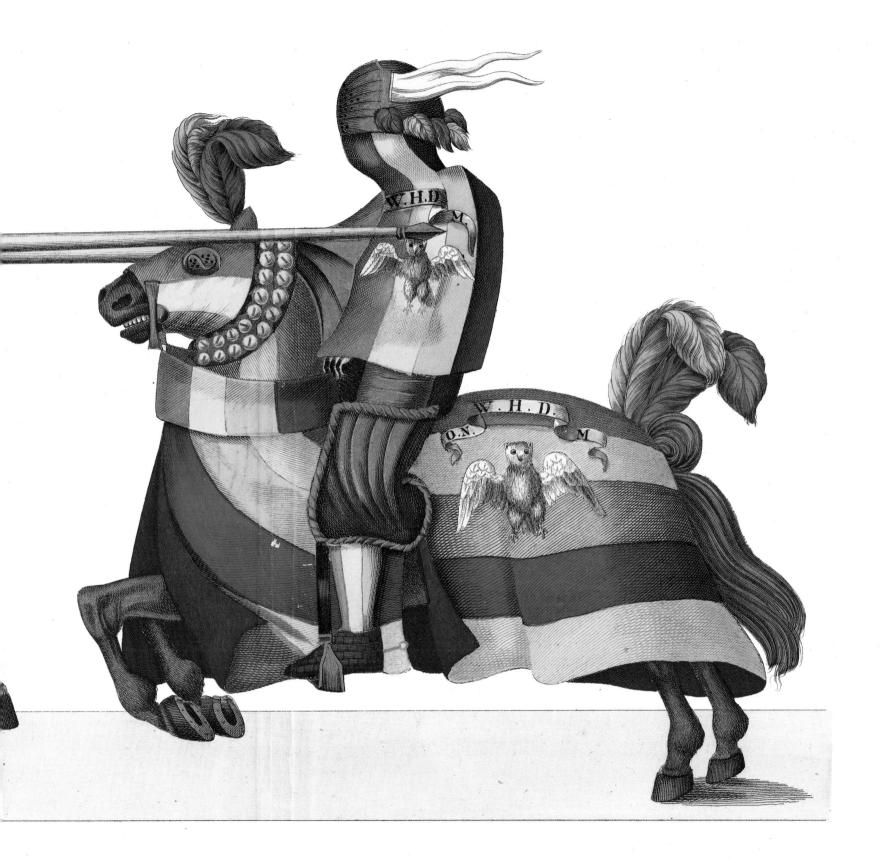

Date Due

FEB 2 4 2004			
OCT – 8 2004			
NOV 0 3 2004			
NOV 1 8 2004			
NOV 1 6 2004			